Think Like God

Think Like God

WARREN HUNTER

DESTINY IMAGE® PUBLISHERS, INC.
P.O. Box 310, Shippensburg, PA 17257-0310
"Speaking to the Purposes of God for this Generation and for the Generations to Come."

This book and all other Destiny Image, Revival Press, Mercy Place, Fresh Bread, Destiny Image Fiction, and Treasure House books are available at Christian bookstores and distributors worldwide.

For a U.S. bookstore nearest you, call 1-800-722-6774.
For more information on foreign distributors, call 717-532-3040.
Reach us on the Internet: www.destinyimage.com.

ISBN 10: 0-7684-2710-X
ISBN 13: 978-0-7684-2710-3

For Worldwide Distribution, Printed in the U.S.A.

1 2 3 4 5 6 7 8 9 10 11 / 12 11 10 09 08

Contents

God created humankind in His image and likeness. God created man to be just like Him in every way. The Lord made man to be His representative, His ambassador, His agent in the earth. God made man to operate in the same manner as God operates, with the same character, nature, and essence as the Father. God made man to mirror back to God every aspect of God in a perfect way. We are created to be a colossal mirror for the Almighty to gaze into. God's heartbeat is for His children to be just like Him. Ephesians chapter 5, verse 1 tells us, "Be imitators of God as dear children. And walk in love, as Christ also has loved us and given Himself for us...." Paul tells the readers of his epistle: imitate the Father like a small child would walk in his daddy's shoes. And don't stop there! Take it to the next level by imitating God the way that Jesus did: by walking in love and sacrificing His life for others. This is a strong message. I am sure many believers today are striving to do just that: to be imitators of God. So let me ask you a personal question: How are you doing with that? Is it going well, or are you struggling?

The reason I ask is simple: though desire and drive to be like God are a good beginning, they are not enough to become like God. Satan desired to be like God and failed miserably. Eve was convinced by the snake that she was not like God and ate of the forbidden fruit to try to attain her goal. Many people follow in their footsteps, walking in pride, self-exultation, and deception, instead of looking to the Maker to find out how to be like Him. God's Word makes it clear that, after purely loving the Lord our God, to be like Jesus should be our number-one goal. God's Word also makes it clear how we are to go about becoming like our Lord and Savior:

> *Let this mind be in you which was also in Christ Jesus, who being in the form of God, did not consider it robbery to be equal with God, but made Himself of no reputation, taking the form of a bondservant, and coming in the likeness of men. And being found in appearance as a man, He humbled Himself and became obedient to the point of death, even the death of the cross* (Philippians 2:5-8).

Let this mind be in you which was also in Christ Jesus. Let me propose to you that becoming like God does not start with what we do. Rather it starts with what we think. Our mind is the great and final battle ground in which the enemy is constantly fighting for a foothold. The question, of course, is, what are we, as God's image bearers, going to do about it? We must decide that we are going to operate in the mind of Christ. This book gives the church a step-by-step plan to overcoming the strongholds of the mind that so many people struggle with. The reader will learn what God intended for our minds and how God plans for us to think as His dear children. Learn to tap into the wisdom that created the universe by meditating on the Word that formed it. You will be touched and forever changed by this radical new look at God's thoughts manifesting in our lives as you are trained how to *Think Like God!*

Chapter One

Wisdom Cries Out

THE AVAILABILITY OF WISDOM

The proverbs of Solomon the son of David, king of Israel:
To know wisdom and instruction,
To perceive the words of understanding... (Proverbs 1:1-2).

The mind of God is a vast universe of wisdom and knowledge, out of which all things were birthed through the channel of His Word. It is true that we were created by a Word from God; however, before God ever spoke the Word that created you, He had thought about you. He meditated on you and how you would be like Him. The Bible says that God's thoughts toward you are more numerous than the sand on the seashore (Psalm 139:17-18). I believe it is our privilege and right as children of God to pursue knowing God's mind in an intimate way. By learning God's thoughts, our minds will be transformed into a place where God's Word can be fully birthed.

In order to begin the process of learning how God thinks, it is important to study what God says. God's Word is the product of God's thought life. That is why God told the writer of Proverbs: as a man thinks in his heart so is He. We know from John chapter 1, verse 1, that God and His Word are one; we can surmise then, that

God's Word would line up exactly with God's thoughts. Jesus confirmed this teaching by telling His followers, "out of the overflow and abundance of the heart the mouth speaks" (Matthew 12:34). God's Word reveals the meditation of God's heart, just as our words reveal what we meditate on. The apostle John tells us in 1 John chapter 5, verse 18, that as He [God] is, so are we in this world; Jesus also told the church that the Kingdom of Heaven had come inside of them. No longer did the earth belong to satan; no longer did his principles rule. Rather God's Kingdom now rules, and God's principles are being enforced by the *Ecclesia*, the called-out ones of God, the Bride of Christ. That means that the principles which operate within God Himself are now operating in and through His children all over the earth. With that said, it should be every Christian's expectation that his or her thought life will become his or her words. As believers, we need to meditate on God's wisdom, so that our minds will be full of God's principles for facing and conquering every situation. God's Word has something to say about every circumstance that humans face every day. For example:

Sickness: Exodus 15:26; Deuteronomy 7:15; Psalm 103:3; Isaiah 53:5; Matthew 4:24, 8:8,13,16[1]

Poverty: Proverbs 6:11, 10:15, 11:24, 13:18, 20:13, 23:21, 24:34, 28:19,22; 30:8, 31:7

Death: Psalm 9:13, 33:19, 48:14, 56:13, 68:20, 89:48, 116:15; Proverbs 8:36, 10:2, 12:28, 18:21

Government: Matthew 22:21, Romans 13:1-4, 1 Timothy 2:1-2, 1 Peter 2:13, 17

Marriage: Genesis 2:23,24, Song of Solomon,

Matthew 19:6, 1 Corinthians 7, Ephesians 5, 1 Timothy 2, 1 Peter 3

As believers, we are not left in the dark as to how God thinks. The Bible and the Holy Spirit were given to us so that we may know for certain what God's will is. We need to study God's wisdom so that we will start to think about our lives in the same way that God thinks about them.

WISDOM CONVEYS THE THOUGHTS OF GOD

The best place to look for God's wisdom is in the Book of Proverbs. The Book of Proverbs wastes no time in giving the reader a clear indication of the great spiritual depths about to be explored. From the beginning its purpose is made clear: "to know wisdom and instruction, to perceive the words of understanding" (Prov.1:2). For many of us, the mere idea that we can understand God's mind and have His understanding is a foreign concept, which carries greater depth then we have ever dared to think about! Yet, according to First Corinthians chapter 2, the Spirit of God searches the deep things of God in order to make known to us what God's will is. God has given us the mind of Christ so that we can trade in the world's way of thinking, speaking, and acting for a higher way—God's way. The author of Proverbs, King Solomon, immediately begins to make his case as to the superiority of God's wisdom over man's shortsighted and often foolish ways.

The concept that God's ways are higher than man's ways is not difficult for people to grasp. All they have to do is look around at the world today to find out that man's ideas about peace, prosperity, truth, love, wisdom, and happiness fail at every turn. Even those who do not claim to be Christians know that man's wisdom is finite and usually self-centered. The problem for most people is grasping the truth that God has made His wisdom available to us. We do not have to continue to use the world's way of thinking, because God has called us to *Think Like God!*

Wisdom has always been perceived as a rare quality, especially among young people. Nevertheless, right from the start Proverbs corrects what is obviously wrong thinking. In the opening chapter, we see the author paint a memorable picture of wisdom crying out in the streets, compelling people to leave behind their simple ways and search after the wisdom and understanding of God.

> *Wisdom calls aloud in the street, she raises her voice in the public squares; at the head of the noisy streets she cries out, in the gateways of the city she makes her speech...* (Proverbs 1:20-21 NIV).

The image of wisdom crying out in the middle of the streets to *anyone* passing by is a bit surprising. In this illustration one would think that such a rare and valuable thing as wisdom would be kept locked away in a storehouse or buried underground like hidden treasure. The impact of the illustration is similar to someone standing on the street corner of a crowded city begging those passing by to accept gold or diamonds, or a suitcase full of money. After all, people are usually searching for these things. And like gold, diamonds, and money, wisdom is always thought of as something that is very difficult to find.

So what is God trying to get across to us in Proverbs 1:20-21?

This Scripture, making clear to us the message of the entire Bible, reveals to us that God is not trying to hide the treasures of His wisdom and understanding from us. Wisdom is, after all, standing in the *public squares*. Wisdom is out in the open trying to get the attention of anyone who will hear her. Therefore, the problem is not the availability of wisdom. Through the power of God's Holy Spirit, we have the ability to know God's wisdom and to emulate His example. The problem is that many people, even some sitting in church pews, are rejecting God's wisdom. In the following verses, notice what God's Word says about those who reject His wisdom:

> *Because they hated knowledge And did not choose the fear of the Lord, they would have none of my counsel and despised my every rebuke* (Proverbs 1:29-31).

Whatever we choose to accept into our lives, the fruit of it will be evident. Those who live by God's Word will bear the fruit of God's Word. Those who live by their own standard or the world's ways of doing things will bear the fruit of the world. What is being emphasized in these verses?

> *They are the ones who hated knowledge,*
> *they failed to choose to fear God,*
> *they rejected and spurned wisdom's rebuke;*
> *they will bear the fruit of their ways.*

The problem does not lie with God. He makes His way plain to anyone who will hear. God has communicated His wisdom in simple ways that even a small child can understand. The problem is not that God's wisdom is scarce or that God is very selective concerning with whom he shares His wisdom. The problem revealed in Proverbs chapter 1 is that many people reject what is freely offered to them by the Lord. *They* reject wisdom.

How is it that so many are failing to receive such a wonderful and freely available gift? Very few people on earth would actually admit that they are rejecting the wisdom of God, yet by choosing to live according to man-made standards, by operating according to worldly principles, they are going against what God has laid out in His Word.

OURS FOR THE ASKING

I believe the answer to the dilemma is found in James. Like

Proverbs, the Book of James is often considered the New Testament's book of wisdom. It is therefore very consistent of the Holy Spirit to inspire James to make the same assertion we found so evident in the first few lines of the Book of Proverbs, in the first chapter of his book:

> *If any of you lacks wisdom, he should ask God, who gives* **generously** *to all without finding fault, and it will be given to him* (James 1:5 NIV).

Just like the author of Proverbs, James immediately begins conveying the availability of God's wisdom. And just as it is in Proverbs, his invitation is wide open, not simply directed to a privileged group or a select few. Verse 5's great promise is free *to any of you who lack wisdom*, thus renewing God's promise of wisdom in the New Covenant, and encouraging all believers to seek the endowment of God's wisdom. If we lack wisdom, all we have to do is pray to receive it.

Consider the wisdom of God as something for the asking!

I think it's safe to say that at one time or another every person on earth would fit into the category of "those who lack wisdom." Yet most of us in need of wisdom would be a bit offended by the simplicity of the next point: anyone lacking in wisdom should **just ask God**.

> Not only does God give us wisdom, He gives:
> generously to all,
> without finding fault.

If we were perfectly honest, we would have to admit that deep

14

down inside we really expect God to be stingy with His wisdom. And not only that, we usually feel guilty about asking for such a thing, knowing that we have not always upheld and conformed to God's standard. Yet, God knew we would be hesitant, and that is exactly why he had James write it this way.

It's not just a coincidence that the opening point of both of the two most cherished books on wisdom, representing both Testaments, is this: In God's Kingdom, and in His way of doing things with mankind, we find ourselves in lack because we do not ask.

Even when we do ask, our requests are usually selfish and wasteful (James 4:2-3). To the end of the request we even tack on the name of Jesus much like saying a password. It reminds me of the kid's game called "Simon says." The leader is constantly giving instructions (touch your toes, clap your hands) but the other children are not supposed to follow them until the leader precedes the instruction with "Simon says." As ridiculous as it sounds, I think some people perceive their relationship with God in that same way. Maybe I'll get the wisdom of God if I remember the password! I've heard some preachers say, "I had the faith to believe for a Rolls Royce." God spoke to me once, however, and told me, "Why don't you have faith to believe that My love will be perfected in you?" This struck me. Jesus said, "Seek first the Kingdom of God, and all the things that the Gentiles seek will be added unto you." When we are filled with all the fullness of God's love, then God will do exceedingly abundantly above all we think or imagine! God knows what we have need of before we even ask. The asking is a way for us to acknowledge the One from whom all true wisdom flows: God. Just believe God and He will give you wisdom.

There is a catch, however. Notice James also states that when we ask, "we must believe and not doubt." This is a chance to exercise our childlike faith and trust in God, and cast aside any double-mindedness. The problem of double-mindedness is one of the enemy's strategies to hinder us from thinking like God. Double-mindedness is a result of listening to the thoughts of the enemy, which oppose the promise of God.

> *Double-mindedness always involves meditating on* *True* *thoughts that pull you away from believing God's Word.*

The double or two minds represent two distinct sets of thoughts pulling in opposite directions. One set of thoughts is directing you to God's promises; the other is trying to create doubt. Did you really hear God correctly, doubt will ask you. The voice of doubt is always going to bring up situations from the past in which it *appears* that God has not kept His promises to the fullest measure. Thoughts like these cause a continual vacillation between believing God's Word and questioning God's faithfulness. An example of this in my own life has to do with the prophetic words which have been spoken over my ministry. One of those prophetic words was that the stadiums of the world would be our pulpit. We have preached in several stadiums in other nations, but have not yet seen the full manifestation of this word. However, we continue to meditate daily on the truth that God will open to us the stadiums of the world. As we do this, we see God open even more doorways to minister across the globe. When you hold on to a prophetic word and meditate on it, then that meditation will move itself into reality.

Notice what James says about this kind of person:

> *But let him ask in faith, with no doubting, for he who doubts is like a wave of the sea driven and tossed by the wind. For let not that man suppose that he will receive anything from the Lord;* (James 1:6-7).

We should not allow opposing thoughts to distort the simple truth in the invitation, "if any of you lacks wisdom, he should ask

God." Memorizing God's promises from Scripture is a great way to reinforce the truth and silence confusion and doubt. Confessing what the Scripture says through memorization will cause all the questioning lies of the enemy to dissipate. When the enemy attacks us with thoughts of doubt, we can answer in the same manner as Jesus answered satan: "It is written!"

RELYING ON GOD

If God wants His wisdom to work in everyone, why should He make us even ask? Why not simply put it in everyone?

Again, by our *acknowledgment* of God as the source of all wisdom (right thoughts), we are confirming that the answer is not coming from within ourselves. We are continually acknowledging God as our source. What God has placed on the inside of every person, however, is the desire to search for wisdom and knowledge. Humans have something inside of them: it is an unquenchable passion to know more today then they did yesterday. The simple truth is that the only thing that can really satiate our desire is intimacy with the All-knowing One. By trusting in Him, we have access to the things our heart is truly seeking. On the other hand, when we fail to trust God, we are putting our trust in ourselves. When we reject God, we really have nowhere to turn but to answers of human origin, which I refer to as *the arm of the flesh*.

This ties in directly with the man of two minds. Sometimes we let what we *naturally* think override what the Holy Spirit wants us to think. The truth is that God's wisdom is contrary to natural, human wisdom. Chapter 1 of First Corinthians teaches that even God's "foolishness" makes man's wisdom look like pure stupidity, and God's "weakness" makes man's strength look like nothing at all. We should expect that when God really begins to move in our lives and speak to and through us, His ways will be beyond our normal comfort zones and areas of knowledge.

17

Think Like God

It is with this in mind that we read the following passage. "For My thoughts are not your thoughts, nor *are* your ways My ways," says the Lord "For *as* the heavens are higher than the earth, so are My ways higher than your ways and My thoughts than your thoughts" (Isaiah 55:8-9).

God's wisdom is contrary to natural, human wisdom.

Like the people of modern society, the people of Isaiah's time had developed thought patterns that were contrary to God's way of thinking and doing things. *They* were the ones responsible for putting a vast distance between themselves and God. God had not chosen to put that space there. It was the children of Israel who were afraid to speak to God and begged Moses to go on their behalf. They did not want to draw near to God, hear His voice, and receive His Word because it meant leaving behind old patterns of thinking and doing things. Notice the prophet's call for repentance just prior to this verse:

> *Seek the Lord while He may be found;*
> *Call on Him while He is near*
> *Let the wicked forsake his way,*
> *And the unrighteous man his thoughts…* (Isaiah 55:6-7a).

The point is that although there is a great distance between the way we think and the way God thinks, we should reject the way we think in favor of the way God thinks. Relying on God's thoughts means not continually reverting to old thinking patterns when we face adversity. When we hit a wall, we should begin to meditate on what God's Word says about that hindrance. Think to yourself, "This mountain is going to become a plain! This mountain is going to be cast into the sea. This wall is going to fall down. God has given me dominion. I can see it just like Joshua could see the wall of Jericho falling in his mind's eye!" Do not let your position of strength and trust in God be made to waver because it looks a little bleak on the outside. God's definition of real reliance on Him starts with the way we think about Him and ourselves.

"Let the evil man forsake his thoughts."

In other words, God is saying, leave the old way of thinking behind and accept my thoughts.

> *Although God's thoughts are higher than ours, His wisdom is still for the asking. If we forsake our old thoughts it's not too late to think like God.*

If this is really the truth, and God's thoughts are available to us through His Word and through intimacy with Him, why do we still struggle to think like Him? Why do we revert to old patterns? I believe the biggest problem we face is that our own flesh is crying out even louder. It is because we have spent a great amount of time listening to the flesh and the thoughts of the enemy and have a history of disobedience to overcome.

For the majority of us, it is now very easy to lean on the arm of the flesh and get caught up with what *we* want to do, instead of calling on God. We have had years of practice. We have also had years of experience doing things based on habits and tradition. We fall into the trap of assuming that because everyone else has done things a certain way, that way must be the right way. We forget that both Jesus and Paul warn us not to be caught up with the traditions of men, which make the Word of God of no effect and keep people from entering the Kingdom of God.

One would think that people in ministry would be the first to avoid this mistake. That's not the case. In reality it seems that an unhealthy dependence on natural thinking and worldly ways of doing things and solving problems has invaded many ministries.

I admit that I have even witnessed this kind of thing firsthand in my own ministry. At times I will be absorbed in the Holy Spirit and walk out of a service excited because the Holy Spirit moved and ministered to the people. Being caught up with Him, I think only of the bigness of God. Later my ministry team and I find out that something didn't happen exactly the way that we *thought* it should. I expect a certain result, and when that result does not manifest, I tend to ask what went wrong. We then begin to analyze the situation. This is when the devil tries to play on our weaknesses and question our obedience to the voice of God. He may say, "Did you really follow the voice of God accurately?" We start to examine all of our decisions and actions, picking them apart for answers. In all actuality, the enemy is trying to create an unnecessary frustration that will distract us from the progress we are making and the lives we are touching. When our motive is love, we can expect *God to work with God,* because love will always take us into the perfect will of God. If our motive was love, then we can expect God's will to come to pass. The truth is, sometimes you need to leave things alone in faith and let God work on what was said. Real reliance on God is knowing that God's wisdom has come out of your mouth and will do the work without any philosophizing, arguing, or analyzing.

Anytime we speak to try to ease frustrations, we give the devil an open invitation, and he immediately goes to work on what was said. At times it may seem beneficial to "air dirty laundry" or to expose the frustrations and irritations we are dealing with; we must be very watchful concerning when, where, and to whom we expose ourselves. The devil is just looking for an opportunity to use negative and unkind words. Before we know it, it comes up again, and we begin to rehash the situation over and over again. The thoughts turn round and round continually, eventually bumping God's thoughts on the matter out. Real reliance on God is choosing not to blurt out words of worry and frustration every time we come up against an issue in our lives; rather we need to choose to release God's thoughts on the

✗ Vital

matter and remain in peace. Satan is just waiting for us to speak angry or frustrated words of doubt. He knows then that we have been meditating on his lies instead of casting them down.

From this example you can see that our enemy specializes in thoughts contrary to God's Word, whether they come directly from him, or whether they are simply naturalistic thinking. He loves to climb on negative thoughts, to ensure that he gets the maximum mileage out of each one. His success is measured on how many of God's thoughts he can squeeze out. He is trying to replace every truth and promise with a seed of deception. When God says, "You are healed," the devil will say, "Are you really? You do not look well. You do not feel well. You do not seem very healthy. Listen to the way you are breathing. And you know it is getting worse! Are you sure God keeps His promises?" If we allow the questions of the devil to ruminate in our minds, if we meditate on His lies, we will end up thinking that the way we think is true, while never realizing that if we changed our thoughts, our circumstances would be immediately altered. By continually going back and forth between God's thoughts and carnal thoughts, we are wasting our time and energy and forgetting to bridle our own mind.

The Spanish Bible has an interesting translation of Proverbs 29:18. It says, "where there is no vision men run around like wild horses." This is a picture of confusion. It is also a picture of wasted potential. Great energy is expended, but for no purpose. To avoid running through life like a wild horse, we all should practice listening to God's thoughts, even if they are contrary to the way things are usually done. As the right thoughts develop into habitual patterns, they are going to solidify and they will produce the right kind of circumstances. But if wrong thoughts develop into wrong habitual patterns, they will solidify into wrong circumstances. If they really are God's thoughts, you can count on them running crossways of traditional thinking. Do not be concerned if God's way of thinking questions a lot of the traditional ways you looked at God before. He wants to break you out of the little box you used to be in and move you into the limitless expanses of who He really is.

Likewise, when we recognize that God's wisdom if freely available, and we put the right value on God's way of thinking, we will find it much easier to forsake the old way of thinking.

The key is in putting more value on God's kind of thinking than on what we know from our past.

> *My son, if you receive My words,*
> *And treasure My commands within you,*
> *So that you incline your ear to wisdom,*
> *And apply your heart to understanding...*
> (Proverbs 2:1-2).

These verses are setting up a pattern of how we are to perceive God's wisdom. When he uses the word *treasure,* he is saying God's commandment is of the utmost value. It is the most important thing that a believer possesses. When we treasure the commandments of God, it changes things. It makes it harder for His thoughts to be replaced or bumped out by wrong thinking.

If a man owned a solid gold watch with real diamonds that he wore every day and treasured, do you suppose it would be difficult for someone to replace it with a $10 watch?

There is unlimited wisdom for the asking.

We can receive the fullness of who God is and His infinite wisdom if we will just ask Him. Ask the Father for wisdom every day because we all need wisdom in order to combat and have victory over the slings and arrows of the enemy. It is very easy for us to lean on the arm of the flesh and get caught up with what we want to do instead of calling on God. But you can change that by meditating on God's words of wisdom both day and night and confessing the truth of God's Word over your life. Sometimes we let what we think override what the Holy Spirit wants to do. Let us practice yielding to the thoughts of God by confessing, "Holy Spirit, I yield to Your way of thinking and doing things. I declare that I have the wisdom of God and that I think the thoughts of God. I refuse to go back to old patterns of thinking and doing from my past." By confessing this daily, we will be putting a stop to the constant vacillation between God's truth and the lies of the devil. People develop patterns of thoughts, thinking "everyone else has always done it this way." Instead, let God do the exact opposite through you. God wants to do a new thing through you that He has never done before. God wants to renew your thoughts and change your thinking.

Think Like God:
GOD-THOUGHTS FOR MEDITATION

- Wisdom conveys God's thoughts.
- Consider God's wisdom as something for the asking!
- Double-mindedness always involves meditating on thoughts that pull you away from believing God's Word.
- God's wisdom is contrary to natural, human wisdom.
- Although God's thoughts are higher than ours, His wisdom is still for the asking. If we forsake our old thoughts, it's not too late to think like God.
- Likewise, when we recognize that God's wisdom is freely available, and we put the right value on God's way of thinking, we will find it much easier to forsake the old way of thinking.

ENDNOTE

1. These lists are not extensive; many other verses exist within both the Old and New Testament pertaining to these areas.

Chapter Two

Shaping Your Future

THE STRONGHOLD OF REJECTION

"Dad, I can't see mom anymore. Slow down so she can catch up!"

I was in a car with my dad just a little way ahead of her. One minute I was watching her follow us. The next minute, I couldn't see her. I told my dad several times to slow down. He kept saying to me, "No, Warren. It's fine. Mom knows the way." I had a feeling in the pit of my stomach, however, that it was not fine. I knew that something very terrible had happened. Even though I was only 6, my spirit told me that we needed to go back and find her. Well, my dad did not go back, and it was not long until what I had sensed was confirmed. We received the news that mom had been killed in a car accident.

I had been very close to my mother because of her great spiritual influence on me. In the first grade, I had learned a lesson about the fires of hell, and afterward I had a great desire to see all my friends saved so they would never have to go there. I would first tell them about Jesus, and then I would bring them to my mother who would lead them in the prayer of salvation. In my first grade year,

I brought over 25 kids to Christ. She was a very important part of my life. I was only 6 when mom died. Somehow, when that happened, I felt all alone in the world. A door was wide open for rejection to enter my life.

I remember years later having to deal with things that resulted from her death. As time went by, thoughts continued to come up in me. Thought patterns centered on rejection and fear constantly fought against what God was doing in my life. Somehow, they were tied to the loss of my mom.

> *The human mind can often settle on ways of dealing with abusive or tragic events that are not only unhealthy, but eventually cause one to accept one lie after another.*

It was not until after I met my wife that the solution to the whole situation became clear. It is amazing how God used her to bring healing by giving her a word of wisdom on the issue. Why did God not give the word to me? Perhaps he had, and I didn't hear it. Whatever the case, too often there are things that we cannot see ourselves, that God is able to open up to another. Sometimes, when things are so close to our own heart, we can more easily allow ourselves to be blinded to the answer. I believe God uses close friends, family members, and especially spouses to bring revelation in this way. That's not to say that the enemy won't try to use them as well to bring confusion. Nevertheless, her words were confirmed in my own spirit. She told me I had never forgiven my mother for dying.

Finally, another person had brought up what I had not been able to bring myself to affirm for nearly twenty years. The Word bore witness within my own spirit because at that point God revealed to me the inward struggle I had been going through. He also made the solution very clear. In order to heal, I had to strike at the root of what satan had sown in my life. I had to release the root cause of what had grown into a mental stronghold of rejection *by forgiving my mom for dying*. In addition, I also had to deal with blaming my dad for driving on ahead and losing sight of my mom. In my mind he was partially responsible for killing her, when in reality he had nothing to do with it.

As a small boy in grief, I had permitted thoughts of blame to circulate and grow. Of course, as a 6-year-old boy, I had no concept of accidents of this type, and deep within I felt a sense of rejection. Indeed, that is exactly why traumatic events or even the suffering of abuse at such an early age can be so devastating.

As my father remarried and tried to move on, things only got worse. I carried rejection into the next few stages of my life, and as I grew, so did the problems. The whole ordeal was never dealt with properly. God's healing power was never brought fully to bear until after my wife's word.

This is not a testimony to the power of the enemy. This is an example of how we often open the door for satan to invade our lives with wrong thought patterns. Just as a lion seeks out the youngest and weakest member of the herd to chase down and devour, satan loves to use experiences like these against young children to plant the mental seeds of a future dysfunctional life. But God always has a solution.

STRIKING THE ROOT

Let me be clear on this. If you have suffered anything like this in the past, do not think for a moment that it is something that can continue to hold you back.

I do not care how bad you have been hurt or abused; God can change it and literally wipe out its power to hold you back.

In my case, the minute I forgave my mother, it made a change in my heart. This heart change caused a chain reaction that eventually corrected the way I received thoughts from God. The channel from God to me was repaired. No doubt satan's stronghold had been very powerful, but God knew how to pull his strongholds down. It doesn't matter how big and tall the tree is, if you cut it down and pull up its roots, it can't receive what it needs to continue to grow and thrive. The roots of satan's tree had been destroyed and that caused his entire tree to collapse.

For as he thinks in his heart, so is he (Proverbs 23:7a).

This verse explains exactly what is wrong with many people today. When we allow certain kinds of thoughts to circulate in our mind, they will eventually grow just like a seed in the ground that is watered and given sunlight. How do they get water and light? We give it to them by loaning them space and energy in our mind. We do it by giving them permission to churn about in our heads. We fail to use our authority and restrict them like we should. That's how we allow them to increase.

We are today what we thought yesterday.

When they increase over time, they actually take root in our heart. Thoughts will continue to grow in our mind, but what we do not realize is that roots are growing deeper and deeper into the depths of our heart. Again, the image of a tree perfectly explains this concept. When a tree is very young, it can be pulled up, because the root system is not really developed. By the time a tree is tall and mature above ground, the system of roots underneath has developed into a massive body demanding more and more resources. I have even heard that with some types of trees the part of the tree underneath can be greater than what is seen above ground. For example, aspens grow in families of trees and share root systems. Likewise, the thoughts we are aware of on the surface may not be telling the whole story of what is underneath. As thoughts become more rooted in the heart, those thoughts turn into habitual patterns of thinking. At this point they are so entrenched on the inside that they will affect the course of our whole life.

Once again, however, from God's point of view, it does not matter how big the stronghold is; He still has the answer. No matter how problematic your childhood may have been, God has never come upon a problem that He does not have the answer to.

THE STRONGHOLD OF NEGATIVITY

Of course, it does not always have to be some traumatic child-hood experience. Satan attempts to affect the thinking of every person on earth regardless of his or her childhood. In fact, many times he has more long-term success on people who have had a relatively normal childhood. This is because they are often less aware of damaging strongholds. They think that because their childhood or upbringing was good, satan could not possibly sow a destructive thought pattern into their life. And since their life seems to be going good on the surface, they cannot see how negative their thought patterns really are.

I remember going to South Africa to hold revival meetings with some friends. On this particular occasion, while ministering, we faced many obstacles. I would leave a meeting right after a powerful service and begin to think and speak negative thoughts as I left. For some reason, it was not going as I thought it should. At that time my friend turned to me and said, "Do you hear what you're saying? You've got to stop talking like that. Stop thinking negatively and start thinking positively. Start thinking the right things." At that time I was speaking out of past rejection. If we speak rejection, we are sowing future rejec-tion into our lives. We have to have a paradigm shift—a correction in the way we think about ourselves. We have to look at ourselves through the eyes of God's Word, not through the eyes of men or our so-called past "failures." If we gaze upon our lives with the negativity created by past issues, we will never be free from them; our lives will continue in a cycle of failure and rejection.

Often, this seems like a small issue to many people, especially compared with a traumatic childhood experience. Nevertheless, I can say from experience that,

Simple negative thought patterns are doing far more to rob people of what God has for them than virtually any other kinds of thoughts.

Negative thoughts are sneaky. I could not figure out why I was thinking negatively. Every time God achieved something big it would seem like something bad was attached to it. Of course, bad things happen. Sometimes we go through a cycle so many times that it gets difficult to break out. It's easy to start saying things like, "Just as soon as we're blessed, we better be ready for the fight of our lives," or "It seems like just as soon as we get ahead, the devil beats us right back down." That proves just how far negative thoughts are permitted to go. Some people who would never allow themselves to think lustful thoughts toward the opposite sex, will spout off in anger in a second. They may be able to think the thoughts of God concerning holiness and purity, but they are unable to uproot the seeds of bitterness and negativity that have taken root in their minds. Instead of repeating the pattern over and over again by meditating on destructive thoughts, we should change the way we talk. Why not say this instead: "Wait a minute; I'm getting ready to take on something big, and something bad *is not* going to happen; it is not going to happen because in my thoughts I won't allow it to happen!" We have trained ourselves to resist thoughts of lust, stealing, or cheating (as well we should have), but we have turned right around and allowed our minds to be used as satan's sewer of negativity. The truth is, negativity opens the door for other thoughts to enter our minds and can be used by the enemy create other cycles of sin.

In the end, it seems that satan has more understanding of the above verse in Proverbs *(as he thinks in his heart, so is he)*, than many Christians. Satan has understood how to affect even our actions by sowing negative thoughts in our heart.

But not only do negative thoughts eventually affect our actions, they also have another devastating effect. When we dwell on the negative, we have negative thoughts blocking what God wants us to think about. They're blocking our solution, even our victory. Negative thoughts block out and replace what He wants us to do.

HEART THOUGHTS WILL SURFACE

"As a man thinks in his heart so is he (Prov. 23:7)." It is very important to understand the setting of this Scripture in order to relate God's thoughts on the subject. Notice the context in the passage below.

> *When you sit down to eat with a ruler,*
> *Consider carefully what is before you;*
> *And put a knife to your throat*
> *If you are a man given to appetite.*
> *Do not desire his delicacies,*
> *For they are deceptive food.*
> *Do not overwork to be rich;*
> *Because of your own understanding, cease!*
> *Will you set your eyes on that which is not?*
> *For riches certainly make themselves wings;*
> *They fly away like an eagle toward heaven.*
> *Do not eat the bread of a miser,*
> *Nor desire his delicacies;*
> *For as he thinks in his heart, so is he.*
> *"Eat and drink!" he says to you,*

But his heart is not with you.
The morsel you have eaten, you will vomit up,
And waste your pleasant words (Proverbs 23:1-8).

"Go ahead, eat and drink." But his *heart* is not with you.

In other words, what you hear coming out of his mouth is not a true indication of what he is like on the inside. All the time he is telling you to eat, but in his heart he resents having to give. The point in all of this is that his true thoughts will eventually surface. His true thoughts have had years to take root; they cannot be hid by a few polite words like, "Go ahead and help yourself, eat and drink all you want." In the end, you will be worse off by accepting his invitation. The evil thoughts that have taken root in his heart will cause him to turn on you.

Believe me; this principle is true in all people's lives. People may be dealing with something on the inside that they think no one can see. They will smile and laugh, but in their hearts they are anxious and depressed, always trying to cover up their true feelings. It is these kinds of people who have ulcers and nervous breakdowns; everything that they are meditating on in their hearts finally comes pouring out in a huge eruption. They can no longer hide, so the exact thing they were afraid would happen really does happen. Whether it is a hurt from the past, or financial difficulties for the present, or anxiety over the future, we need to come clean before God, expose our hurts, worries, and anxieties, and allow God to replace our thoughts with His thoughts.

ESTABLISH THE RIGHT PATTERN

God's thoughts are always geared toward the power of His Word coming to pass in people's lives. He is focused on our inevitable success, not failure. This is the way I want to think about myself also. On many occasions I have been in a service ministering and my thoughts would begin to flow in line with God's Word. God would begin to give His thoughts of what should happen in that service. Before I would even pray for someone, I would begin thinking that the power of God is going to touch him or her in a certain way. In my mind I would eventually see it happening. Sometimes you may even start off struggling, but once the pattern is established, everything flows smoothly. Finally, when you pray for the person, that person is healed. As you think God's thoughts, they become established; as they become established, they manifest.

This is not some kind of mental exercise, mind-control, or mind-over-matter thing. This is applying the truth of God's Word. This is simply cooperating with what God has for us. This is true obedience.

God knows how *effective* thoughts can be; in fact, He created them to operate like they do for a reason.

Even the cycle of thinking that begins to take root deep in our mind was created for a purpose. It was meant for *God's thoughts* to take root and become established, not for the strongholds of the enemy. Remember that *strongholds* of the enemy are not evil powers over cities, or ruling countries. According to Scripture, strongholds are in the mind. Notice what it says about strongholds in Second Corinthians:

> *For the weapons of our warfare are not carnal but mighty in God for the pulling down of strongholds, casting down arguments and every high thing that exalts itself against the knowledge of God, bringing every thought into captivity to the obedience of Christ...* (2 Corinthians 10:4-5).

Satan knows how powerful your cycle of thinking is. That is exactly why he attempts to set up strongholds in your mind. That is also why we have to cast down every thought that is not in harmony with God's thoughts.

Choose Your Thoughts Carefully

Thoughts affect all of our being. They extend out into the situations and circumstances of our life. They affect every aspect of a person's life. God has placed within us the ability to choose the way our thoughts will go. Our thoughts are not dictated to us by our circumstances; rather it is the other way around. Our thoughts will either take us in the direction of success or in the direction of failure. Our words will be the direct product of our thoughts, and by our words, our actions will be dictated to. The actions we perform will decide the habits we will form, and the habits we form will become our lifestyle of choice. Our lifestyle will become our eternity. It is up to us.

People respond to others based on what they have meditated upon.

Take a look at these instructions from Proverbs. Notice the emphasis placed on what enters the heart:

> *My son, give attention to My words;*
> *Incline your ear to My sayings.*
> *Do not let them depart from your eyes;*
> *Keep them in the midst of your heart;*
> *For they are life to those who find them,*
> *And health to all their flesh.*
> *Keep your heart with all diligence,*
> *For out of it spring the issues of life.*
> *Put away from you a deceitful mouth,*
> *And put perverse lips far from you* (Proverbs 4:20-24).

The heart in the Bible often represents a person's inner self wherein lies that person's deepest thoughts. That is why the author of

Proverbs writes, "keep your heart with all diligence, for out of it spring the issues of life."

What are the issues of *your* life?

What is going to direct your life?

What is going to guide your life and bring you success or failure, blessing or cursing?

Thoughts enfold all of our existence and reach out to all the conditions and circumstances of our lives. Thoughts cover every aspect of a person's life. Like seeds in the natural, they grow until they impact our whole life.

In 1959 James Allen published a fascinating book entitled *As a Man Thinketh*. In it he makes this same analogy:

> As the plant springs from and could not be without the seed, so every act of man springs from hidden seeds of thought and could not have appeared without them. The supply is equal to those acts called spontaneous and unpremeditated as to those, which are deliberately executed.[1]

In other words, the results are still the same whether we intend to act a certain way or whether we think we are acting spontaneously. Our actions still carry the same results. The results depend on the meditation of our heart. Whether you think you are acting in a deliberate way or a spontaneous way, *what you have been thinking about still effects the outcome.*

By the right of choice, true application of the thoughts of God is what is going to take us in the right direction to bring us into all that God has for us.

How many times have you stuck your foot in your mouth?

How many times have you said something that you would have given anything to take back if you could?

All those times were the results of your thought life. When you make the right choices and choose God's thoughts, God can affect even the things that you say on the spur of the moment. As a man thinks, so is he.

Choose your thoughts carefully.

THE PATHWAY

The Spirit Himself bears witness with our spirit that we are children of God (Romans 8:16).

This is something God is trying to encourage in our lives. He wants us to act like Him; that is why He sent His Word and His Son, as an example of the right way to think and act. When we begin to think and speak anointed words, it will cause our full relationship with our Father to manifest.

What we think will eventually come to pass.

This is meant to be a good thing, not a bad thing. God's design is to establish a clear pathway from His heart to our life. *In that pathway, our mind is in the center.*

If you truly believe you are a son of God, you will gear your consciousness toward that.

Relying on His thoughts is very important in order for us to receive more of what He has for us. **To trust and lean on the thoughts of God is the key to receiving more.** But be warned. Anytime that we claim the exclusive rights to thoughts that originated from Him, we get into ego. We are basically saying that we did it. In other words, if we claim credit, God has to pull back, and eventually our own thoughts are again manifesting, leading to failure. Our thoughts will be the only source we can pull from, thereby showing the definite limitations of the human intellect. By denying our source, we are hindering the correct flow of the pathway God established. But when we rely solely on the Holy Spirit and God's Word, we are actually allowing a channel to be created between God's mind and our own. Remember, Jesus was and is the most humble man that ever lived; He is also the one who said, "I and My Father are one," and, "The Father loves the Son, and shows Him all things that He Himself does...." Jesus was full of confidence because He knew who His source was.

Even though our motives might be correct, we have to watch carefully that our flesh does not try to get in the limelight, instead of giving God the glory. Sometimes, when I talk to pastors on the phone, I will begin to tell them all the mighty acts that God has done through me in revival meetings. Even though my motive is to help them see God's power, my words can be mistaken at times unintentionally as pointing toward the man instead of pointing toward the Father. I get excited and start telling about all the miracles that happen in our services. But it should never be our intent to draw attention to ourselves. Thoughts of "I, Me, and My" will try to draw attention to the flesh. That is why we all have to continually cast down these kinds of thoughts.

*I can only minister to you what I draw
from the grace of God.*

We have to continually discipline our thoughts and our flesh. We have to take up our cross daily and say it is no longer I that live but Christ that lives within me.

Personally, I am trying not to convey my own thoughts but to convey what the Holy Spirit is really trying to say. To catch the pattern of the Holy Spirit is not an easy process. It is a renewing process. In the same way, it may take you a while to get your mind geared in the direction of the supernatural. It does not happen overnight. God wants to rework this pattern of thinking. There is an awesomeness about God that He is setting in your consciousness and your mind that encompasses the vastness of the expanse of the universe. Jesus as a man has covered this vastness of the expanse of the universe; that means He has set up a pattern of success that we as joint-heirs can just step into whenever we choose. We are partakers of unlimited resources because Jesus created a way where there was none. He made it possible for regular people who become part of God's covenant to think like God, speak like God, and act like God—in complete righteousness.

GOD'S THOUGHTS DESTROY THE BARRIER OF TRADITION

A lot of people hear things today that they have never heard before. That means new revelation is coming forth that has never been taught before; songs are being written that carry a different sense of God's presence and power. The old ways of doing things—what some people call "old time revival"—no longer meet the spiritual needs or desires of a new generation! God's "consistent pattern of doing things" is to keep His Word by showing Himself mighty to every generation. God is still doing a new thing—which definitely messes with people's religious ideas about what God can and cannot do.

This is not always bad. Especially given the fact that just like Jesus when He came to earth, we have to break previous patterns, philosophies, traditions, and ideas of human origin that block the supernatural from flowing.

Notice Jesus' encounter with some of the Pharisees in the Book of Mark:

So the Pharisees and teachers of the law asked Jesus, "Why don't Your disciples live according to the tradition of the elders instead of eating their food with 'unclean' hands?"

He replied, "Isaiah was right when he prophesied about you hypocrites; as it is written: 'These people honor Me with their lips, but their hearts are far from Me. They worship Me in vain; their teachings are but rules taught by men.'

You have let go of the commands of God and are holding on to the traditions of men" (Mark 7:5-8 NIV).

It's easy to see from this passage how traditions interfere with the supernatural. The Pharisees were so caught up in their own traditions that they actually went so far as to let go of the true commands of God. They had the supernatural Son of God in their midst, and all they could do was argue about traditions. They were jealous of the favor of God on Jesus' life, of His miracles, signs and wonders, and of how the people followed Him. They used their traditions to quench their desire for the things of God. They allowed traditional ways of thinking to interfere with what God had for them.

> *Even now there are things that God wants to get across to us. Each individual has a unique calling, and God desires to do something special through each of us.*

How exciting it is to think that we are in covenant relationship with an immortal, resurrected man. God is setting up a consciousness in our minds that encompasses the vastness of the universe. God is trying to take us there if we will let go of natural ways of thinking. He is leading the way.

We must be on guard against things that short-change the high calling of God. For example, I know of ministers getting thoughts through media that are not God's thoughts. They get up and minister sermons after they get inspiration from secular media. I hope you realize that the media mixture of philosophy does not often convey the true wisdom or the depth of the Spirit of God.

What it amounts to is this: the Body of Christ is fighting ideas that the world is trying to set up. I am reminded of the time when God's people disobeyed and put the Ark of the Covenant on an oxcart for transportation. God specifically told them it was to be carried by the priests for a reason (see Numbers 4:10-15). Likewise, ministers should not try to convey the spiritual truths of God's Word through the humanistic mixture of secular media. We need to allow God's thoughts to change our minds so that we no longer identify with the world's way of thinking. If we want the thoughts of God in our life, then we have to pursue the depths of God.

> *Beware lest anyone cheat you through philosophy and empty deceit, according to the tradition of men, according to the basic principles of the world, and not according to Christ. For in Him dwells all the fullness of the Godhead bodily; and you are complete in Him, who is the head of all principality and power* (Colossians 2:8-10).

> *See to it that no one carries you off as spoil or makes you yourselves captive by his so-called philosophy and intellectualism and vain deceit (idle fancies and plain nonsense) following human tradition, (men's ideas of the material rather than the spiritual world), just crude, notions following the rudimentary and elemental teachings of the universe and disregarding [the teachings of] Christ (the Messiah)* (Colossians 2:8 AMP).

We are complete in Him, and He will lead our entire thought process if we permit it. But we will never experience the fullness of the power of God with traditions of men and philosophies blocking us.

In our everyday lives, there are thoughts God is constantly trying to get us to receive. We have to permit these thoughts so that we can have the right results. We are the masters of our own thoughts and the molder of our character mainly because God will never force us to take His thoughts. In our own humanity, we have the capacity to receive the right thoughts or the wrong thoughts. Nothing is left to chance. God will lead us, but we must choose His thoughts. We must take responsibility for our own thought life.

When we allow input that will produce, we will bring forth fruit. Bearing fruit will change our character and cause us to bring about a change in our circumstances.

> *Yes, if you cry out for discernment,*
> *And lift up your voice for understanding,*
> *If you seek her as silver,*
> *And search for her as for hidden treasures;*
> *Then you will understand the fear of the Lord,*
> *And find the knowledge of God.*
> *For the Lord gives wisdom;*
> *From His mouth come knowledge and understanding;*
> *He stores up sound wisdom for the upright;*
> *He is a shield to those who walk uprightly...* (Proverbs 2:3-7).

> *When wisdom enters your heart,*
> *And knowledge is pleasant to your soul,*
> *Discretion will preserve you;*
> *Understanding will keep you...* (Proverbs 2:10-11).

It never ceases to amaze me how some people think character in our leadership is not as big a deal as how they stand on certain issues. But the truth is, a person's character is exactly what makes them choose the right issues, because one's character is the product of a certain pattern of thinking. Let's take, for example, the character trait of self-control. Anybody who has practiced self-control for any length of time will notice that the change in his circumstances has been in equal proportion with the change in his thought life. The alteration of our circumstances is the result of thoughts that have developed and solidified into character traits and eventually produced circumstances. This is exactly what happened to you when you were growing up.

> *Every thought is a seed sown; it falls into the ground*
> *of the mind, and will take root sooner or later and*
> *blossom into action.*

As a child you were taught that certain ways of thinking and acting were wrong. When you committed an act that was considered wrong by the authorities in your life, the "right" way of thinking and acting were reinforced in you through discipline. Through this cycle of receiving training, acting upon what you knew, and receiving correction, certain character traits that were deemed important by your parents slowly became part of everyday behavior until these became the essence of who you are. Some of the things parents teach are obvious even at a young age: do not steal, do not hit; be respectful to your elders; treat others as you would like to be treated. Yet there are well-hidden thinking patterns that your parents received from their parents, which have been passed down from generation to generation that they also tried unknowingly to pass on to you. For example, perhaps Great-Grandmother Irene died of a heart attack; so did Grandmother Louise, and your mother, Alice, has very high cholesterol and talks constantly about how it is quite inevitable that she also will lose her life to the deadly heart disease. Your whole life you were informed that the likelihood of you receiving high cholesterol from your ill-fated genes was very high, and that you ought to be very careful.

The idea that you are somehow predestined to die young because of genetic frailty may seem very drastic to you as an example of thought patterns that are learned and solidify into character traits. Yet I am telling you that through just such circumstances, children are being taught that sickness is inevitable; they are taught to live in fear and to talk about their fears all the time. They lose their carefree and innocent nature, replacing it with a spirit of fear and worry. In the same manner, however, godly character traits such as patience, gentleness, and self-control can be cultivated by practicing a thought life that is focused on God and His thoughts.

If you start practicing self-control in your thoughts and receive the purification of the Holy Spirit, a change will be made, and when you change your thoughts, you will begin to change your circumstances.

Pure thoughts produce pure fruit.
Impure thoughts produce impure fruit.

An example of this is in the area of worship.

WORSHIP AND THOUGHTS

Worshiping God requires great discipline in the thoughts. When a person worships God, his or her mind is geared to giving honor and glory to Him. Some people have trouble worshiping God because their minds are obsessed with physical addictions like smoking or over-eating. Their minds struggle to give God honor and lordship in their lives because they have given honor and lordship to an idol instead of God. When they come into a worship setting, they remain distant, unwilling to draw near to God so that they can change. However, in order for us to fully receive the things of the Spirit, we have to cultivate worship of the true and living God instead of wasting time in worship of ourselves and/or deaf and dumb idols. When we truly give God adoration from the depth of our hearts, this becomes an incredible bridle for our thoughts.

I have experienced the power of this truth in my own life. One time I was attacked by headaches. I had dealt with this in the past, and had used different means to step into healing. I tried to confess the Word, saying, "I have the mind of Christ." I also tried to lay hands on my head and release the anointing. In the past, these ways of changing my thinking had worked to bring about healing. This time, none of these things worked. The Holy Spirit was trying to teach me the power of arresting my thought through worship. He told me, "Sing love songs to Jesus." Therefore, I began to sing, though I was in much pain and it was quite difficult. As I sang, my thoughts became focused on God's love and goodness, and the pain that was all over my body began to leave until it was completely gone.

Prophetic worship helps us experience the very heartbeat of the Father, thus expressing His thoughts.

Thoughts will give birth to ideas, and ideas will give birth to actions. We begin to recognize that worshiping God helps to align our thoughts correctly. Sadly enough, the reverse of this is often true. People try to worship God in ways that they believe will please God due to preconceived ideas, but they are not truly worshiping God. They are either doing useless actions that they think will make God love them more, or they are doing nothing to show God love because they refuse to move outside of their comfort zones.

This is plainly the difference between religious worship and true worship. Jesus said in John chapter 4, verse 23, "A time is coming and has now come when the true worshipers will worship the Father in spirit and truth, for they are the kind of worshipers the Father seeks." True worship is birthed in the Spirit and is full of truth. Religious worship takes place when people try to please God by leaning on the arm of the flesh instead of leaning on the Spirit.

Leaning on the arm of the flesh entails blatantly refusing to move outside our particular comfort zones in order to please God. If we continue to worship in ways that are familiar to us, even though we feel God tugging on our hearts to move in a new direction, we are leaning on the arm of the flesh and are not entering into true worship. Prophetic worship of God entails seeking God's face to find out what His heartbeat is, and then doing it with self-abandonment! Prophetic worship is when we tap into the mind of Christ to worship God in God's way; we are listening to what God thinks about Himself and about us, which draws us deeper and deeper into His heart.

True worship is when we tap into what the Spirit of God is saying about God. Worshiping God is about finding out what ministers to God, not what is comfortable for us. That is why I always say, when you are preaching the Word to the body, worship God with your message. God's opinion is the only one that really matters. Releasing love to God turns our hearts toward God's goodness and our inevitable victory! Worship helps to make adjustments in our thoughts.

THE MOUTH AND THOUGHTS

Wisdom is found on the lips of him who has understanding,
But a rod is for the back of him who is devoid of understanding.
Wise people store up knowledge,
But the mouth of the foolish is near destruction (Proverbs 10:13-14).

The heart of the wise teaches his mouth,
And adds learning to his lips (Proverbs 16:23).

Why did the writer of Proverbs make this statement? "The heart of the wise teaches his mouth." What comes out of your mouth is the result of thoughts. The heart of the wise is saying, "Hold on; bridle your thoughts. Get your thoughts under control. Speak the right thoughts, because they are going to produce results." The wise man or woman has trained his or her heart to listen carefully and discern where the thoughts are coming from; this person asks him or herself, "Is that thought of the Spirit, the flesh, or the devil?" They realize that if a certain thought is not of God and they choose to meditate on it, it will eventually taint their words. They recognize that death and life is in the power of the tongue.

The tongue of the wise uses knowledge rightly,
But the mouth of fools pours forth foolishness (Proverbs 15:2).

A wholesome tongue is a tree of life,
But perverseness in it breaks the spirit (Proverbs 15:4).

The lips of the wise disperse knowledge,
But the heart of the fool does not do so (Proverbs 15:7).

Thus, the pathway ordained by God is like this:

1. Thoughts are like the seeds of actions.
2. Like a seed, your thoughts are planted and develop in the ground of your mind.
3. What comes out of your mouth is in large part the result of your thoughts.
4. Meditation is like giving the seeds sunshine.
5. As you reinforce your thoughts with the words that you choose to speak, the seeds are watered.
6. And when the seed matures, it changes your actions.

7. Therefore, the heart of the wise gets his thoughts under God's control.

The thoughts of the wicked are an abomination to the Lord,
But the words of the pure are pleasant (Proverbs 15:26).

The heart of the righteous studies how to answer,
But the mouth of the wicked pours forth evil (Proverbs 15:28).

The heart of the righteous always thinks about what it is going to say before it speaks! He does not merely blurt out the way he feels or the severity of his circumstances. Rather, he speaks the words which he knows will please the Father.

Man is the master of his thoughts and the molder of his character, but the answer of the tongue should come from the Lord. Even though God has given man the ability to choose right from wrong and whom he will serve, each man must consider the outcome of his choice. If he is wise, he will allow the Lord to rule in his mind and mouth, so that the Lord, not his flesh, determines his circumstances.

The preparations of the heart belong to man,
But the answer of the tongue is from the Lord....
Commit your works to the Lord,
And your thoughts will be established....
Everyone proud in heart is an abomination to the Lord;
Though they join forces, none will go unpunished
(Proverbs 16:1, 3, 5).

Pride is rooted in wrong-thinking patterns. When we do not commit our works to the Lord, we rely on our own strength, which is the groundwork for prideful thoughts. Pride develops when true knowledge is missing. When we do not have a clear understanding of our righteousness in the Lord, we will look at ourselves through our own expectations, talents, and so-called successes. The Bible teaches us to look at ourselves in a sober manner and not think of ourselves as higher then we ought. If we commit our ways to the Lord and remain dependent on Him to bring His Word to pass in our lives, then pride will not be able to have a stronghold in our lives. If we allow the Holy Spirit to make an adjustment to how we think about ourselves, then pride will be destroyed by righteous thoughts.

> *Let heaven fill your thoughts. Do not think only about things down here on earth. For you died when Christ died, and your real life is hidden with Christ in God* (Colossians 3:2-3 TLB).

Let Heaven fill your thoughts! Let *God-thoughts* fill your mind! Remember, Jesus prayed, "Your Kingdom come, Your will be done, on earth as it is in Heaven." We want Kingdom thoughts to be established on earth. The only way they are going to be established in us is if we possess the Kingdom thoughts and convey them. We have to speak them out into this earth. We have to speak forth the restoration of God's will on earth. We have to speak forth God's dominion. We have to speak forth the authority of God over this earth. We have got to get the thoughts of God in order to bring the words of Jesus to pass. In order to break and alter the pattern of sin and death, in order to break the control of the one who *had* the power over death—that is, satan—we have got to begin to let *God's thoughts dominate in us.*

Think Like God:
GOD-THOUGHTS FOR MEDITATION

- The human mind can often settle on ways of dealing with abusive or tragic events that are not only unhealthy, but eventually cause one to accept one lie after another.
- I don't care how bad you've been hurt or abused; God can change it and literally wipe out its power to hold you back.
- You are today what you thought yesterday.
- Simple negative thought patterns are doing far more to rob people of what God has for them than virtually any other kinds of thoughts.
- We have to cast down every thought that is not in harmony with God's thoughts.
- People respond to others based on what they have meditated upon.
- By the right choice, true application of the thoughts of man is what's going to take you in the right direction to bring you to perfection.
- We have to break previous patterns, philosophies, traditions, and ideas of human origin that block the supernatural from flowing.
- Every thought is a seed sown; it falls into the ground of the mind, and will take root sooner or later and blossom into action.

ENDNOTE

1. James Allen. *As a Man Thinketh* (St. Augustine, FL: AsaManThinketh.net. 2001), 5.

Chapter Three

An Anointed Mind

CHRIST-CONSCIOUSNESS

Have you ever heard the saying, "You are so heavenly minded that you are no earthly good"? Usually it is said of people who are supposedly so caught up in God that they are no good to anyone on earth. In other words, they have such a one-track mind that they can't really be of help in practical areas. But that statement shows you just how messed up our thinking is on this whole issue. The truth is, the more heavenly minded you are, the more earthly good you will be!

The whole thing reminds me of the story of Martha and Mary in the Gospel of Luke:

> *Now it happened as they went that He entered a certain village; and a certain woman named Martha welcomed Him into her house. And she had a sister called Mary, who also sat at Jesus' feet and heard His word. But Martha was distracted with much serving, and she approached Him and said, "Lord, do You not care that my sister has left me to serve alone? Therefore tell her to help me."*

And Jesus answered and said to her, "Martha, Martha, you are worried and troubled about many things. But one thing is needed, and Mary has chosen that good part, which will not be taken away from her" (Luke 10:38-42).

I can imagine Martha saying to Mary, "You're so heavenly minded that you're no earthly good!"

This is exactly why we have to develop *Christ-consciousness*. This means that our thoughts become sensitive to the flow of the anointing through our lives. *Christ-consciousness is a pattern of behavior that centers on thinking anointed thoughts that create anointed words that produce anointed results.* We have to be able to recognize how little sayings like "They are so heavenly-minded that they are no earthly good" are really opposed to the things of God. The truth of the matter is that Mary had her priorities right. She knew that the Anointed One, the Christ, was sitting right in front of her. She recognized that His Words were anointed, and she wanted to know His thoughts and hear His Words. There was nothing wrong with meeting the physical needs of Jesus and the disciples, provided she did not put that above the Word of God. Mary recognized what was important. In truth, the more heavenly minded a person becomes, the more earthly good they will be. Our focus on God and His Word will enable us to be salt and light to all the people around us.

Now apply this to the areas of the thought life. Recall the part of our Lord's prayer that states, "Your Kingdom come, Your will be done on earth as it is Heaven...." The saying about being so heavenly minded that you're no earthly good is actually contrary to this Scripture. To be of any earthly good, we have to establish God's Kingdom in some way. We have to speak forth the authority of God on this earth. That is the only way to be of any earthly good. But in order to do that, we have to be more heavenly minded. Thus, it is more accurate to say, the more heavenly minded you are, or the more *Christ-conscious* you are, the more right your priorities will be, and the more earthly good you will be. Your thoughts will be anointed, and your words will be the Word of God; they will produce miracles, signs, and wonders because they are wrapped with the nature of God. Isaiah chapter 10, verse 27 says that the anointing oil removes burdens and destroys yokes. If we think anointed thoughts and speak anointed words, we will see God break the bondages of satan off of people's lives right before our eyes.

When we are *Christ-conscious* and we allow the thoughts of God to transform our minds, we will see the old patterns of thinking such as the pithy statement about "being no earthly good" broken. These old patterns of thinking are created by a continual cycle of thinking just the way we are taught to think and never finding out whether what we think lines up with the Word of God or not. It is as if we were robots, programmed to all function the same way. How horrible this is if the way we were originally programmed was not according to the master design. Some things have been twisted and altered from the perfect mold, and now there are imperfections of thought and action being perpetuated from generation to generation. The only way this can be stopped is if we return to the Master and His plan and allow Him to reprogram us in the fashion of the original and perfect Copy (to find out more about this subject, please listen to the tape "The Master Copy," available at swordministries.org).

The cycle goes something like this: Christians go to Scripture to back up what they believe is right. However, they don't recognize that in the back of their minds they take this theory or philosophy as truth already, which has been passed down through the spirit of deception and really has no scriptural foundation. As a result of these deceptions, what they take from Scripture is slanted to a worldly perspective. They allow their own distorted conscience to dictate what God's Word should be for a particular situation.

A perfect example of this would be the way that certain cults twist and change certain passages in the Scripture to fit their own unscriptural beliefs. One of the common passages that they change is John

1:1: "In the beginning was the Word, and the Word was with God, and the Word was God." The Jehovah's Witnesses Bible reads, "and the Word was a god." This completely changes the meaning of the verse. The word which we translate as "God" in verse one, is the Greek word *Theos*.[1] Although in this context it does not have the definite article preceding it, this word is clearly drawing a direct link between the Father and the Word. Theos is used often in the New Testament to signify the One and Only True God. In the context of the first verse, it is clearly showing us the divinity of the Word in relationship to the Father. The divine Word became flesh, and through Jesus, who is divine, we see all of who the Father is; we behold His glory, full of grace and truth (see John 1:14). If we translate the word *Theos* as "a god," it puts Jesus on the same plane as the gods of the Gentiles, who are also called *theos* at different places in the New Testament. We know however that these gods are no gods at all, and do not have divine origin. They were never with God in the beginning. They are not Divine. Therefore, this translation downplays Jesus' divinity and His relationship with the Father God. The Jehovah's Witnesses translate in this way to legitimize their belief that Jesus is not God.[2]

Some of the Scriptures people pull out of context to try to denounce a legitimate move of the Spirit. Let's say God is moving in their church, but something is done that they don't like. So they pull some Scripture out of context and declare, "This could not be from God because I'm confused, and God is not the author of confusion." The truth is they are confused because they have made an idol out of their own peculiar traditions and expectations. They are confused because their box is being stretched, not because what they are seeing is really out of order. Many times people will at first reject what they have never seen before. New things tend to scare people. New things do not scare God, however. Remember, Psalms says, every time God breathes all the hosts of Heaven come into place (see Psalm 33:6). He is constantly doing something new! This is our inheritance as His children.

THE BLOOD OF JESUS CLEANSES
OUR CONSCIENCES

A similar situation existed in the early church. The people the author of Hebrews was addressing had allowed their traditions to supplant the new things that God was doing. They had allowed a system of works to become such a habit that when God showed them more revelation on it, their conscience actually rejected it. This shows that even their consciences had to be cleansed. The traditions and philosophies of the past had become dead works that created a barrier between them and God's Word. Dead works can hinder us from thinking God's thoughts because they are distracting and binding. People tend to reject anything new that comes along that is contrary to the normal pattern of thought flow already established.

That is one reason we have the blood of Christ. It purges our conscience from dead works. The cleansing nature of His blood makes our covenant with God so powerful. The blood has the ability to destroy every hostile and dividing wall between us and God. If they are not cleansed away, dead works will actually multiply and begin a slow take-over of a person's whole mind. The blood of the covenant can purge our conscience from dead works, allowing us to have a pure conscience to hear clearly from God and declare the answers of the Lord. First Timothy 3:9 says that the way that we hold on to the mysteries of faith is with a pure conscience. Let me emphasize again the words, *a pure conscience.* We need the blood of Jesus to purge every dead work so that we can hold on to the mysteries of faith and serve the living God. We need to declare the work that has been done by Jesus on our behalf.

When I declare the answers of the Lord in the Spirit, it is no longer my traditions or philosophies speaking, but the Holy Spirit. I can be assured those answers that I am speaking are from the mind and heart of God.

How much more shall the blood of Christ, who through the eternal Spirit offered Himself without spot to God, cleanse your conscience from dead works to serve the living God? (Hebrews 9:14)

Traditional ways of thinking tied to the world will still try to rise up against the voice of the Spirit. When they do, we need to take authority over them. We need to declare that the blood of Christ has done its work. We do that by thanking the Lord for purging our conscience from all dead works.

Pray this prayer with me:

"I thank You, Father, that the blood of Jesus Christ destroys every hostile wall that separates me from You. I thank You that the blood of Jesus Christ purges my conscience from all dead works to serve the living God! I declare that I have a pure conscience and can hold on to the mysteries of faith. I declare that I have the mind of Christ. I declare that I think like my Father God. I declare that I talk like my Father God. I declare that I act like my Father God. I declare that the thoughts of God dominate me. I declare that the consciousness of God rules and reigns in me. I thank You, Father, for setting me free from all vain and empty traditions and philosophies of men that make Your Word of no effect. In Jesus' name, Amen!"

SHAPING YOUR ENVIRONMENT

Imagination Destination

Every thought is seed sown. When it is allowed to fall into the mind it will take root and produce its own kind sooner or later. Like seeds, thoughts produce according to their kind. When we think

God-size thoughts, we are going to get a God-size result. We need to learn how to better tap into God's vast imagination!

When God created the first man and woman, He created them to be just like Him. That means they did everything as if it were God doing it, and not them at all. There was no separation between God and them. They had perfect communion together all the time. The reason for this is because that first couple had a mind like God—untainted by sin. Just think of it! God's imagination was so big that His meditation became the whole universe. These first humans thought in the exact same manner. They were full of "original thoughts" because they had the creative mind of God within them. Their imaginations were limitless to think up new and exiting worlds with animals and plants that had never existed before. They could imagine flying through galaxies and jumping from planet to planet. Not only could they imagine it, but they could also put their imagination into practice, just as God did when He created the earth. God meditated on light. So when He spoke, "Light, be!" light actually appeared and shown for the very first time. In the same way, the first man named every animal.

God gave us an imagination to grasp and focus on His bigness. Too many people waste their God-given imagination on things that have no value spiritually. Rich businessmen sit around and think up ideas to produce more funds for their own pockets, not for the Kingdom of God. Men and women alike fantasize about fornicating and committing adultery, thinking that no one will ever know. They reason to themselves that it does not hurt anyone because it is just a thought. They have not been taught that whatever they meditate on will take dominion in their life. Then some preacher comes along and lays them under condemnation for thinking evil thoughts but never offers the real reason why carnal thinking is such an affront to God and to who we really are as children of God. Some preachers don't realize that the reason those kinds of lustful fantasies are so wrong is because they are replacing something God wants us to be thinking about. Those carnal ideas are crowding out godly imaginations and creative ideas that would produce huge results for the Kingdom of God.

Satan works so hard sowing thoughts like these because he does not want us to dwell on what God has for us. Satan knows that when we fill our thoughts with godly opportunities, it will eventually lead to a change in our circumstances.

TRANSFORMING YOUR CIRCUMSTANCES— ONE THOUGHT AT A TIME

Your circumstances show you who you really are because your thoughts got you there. The Lord will manifest Himself through the thoughts of a man who allows the Lord our God to master his thoughts. However, if we do not allow the Lord to master our thoughts, how do we expect the Lord to manifest through our thoughts? In other words, let us say that your mind is a conduit—a large pipeline by which something is transmitted—and the something being transmitted is God's Word. If the conduit is full of garbage, whatever form, than the fluid will not be able to flow through it easily to reach its destination. If we would like God's thoughts to manifest in power in our lives to minister God's Word to other people, we have to have a clean channel, not one that is full of other kinds of thoughts and activity.

Circumstances do not determine your outcome; your situation reveals your meditation.

The Lord will manifest through a person who allows Him to be master of his thoughts. That person will become the shaper and author of his environment, because he will be choosing to release God's thoughts out of his mouth. If you think you are a child of God, then you will shape your environment according to a child of God mentality. If you walk as a child of God and believe that you have absolute dominion and authority to operate in the supernatural, the supernatural will occur in your life.

The thoughts we send out, we will receive back multiplied.

The truth is that we usually do not recognize the consequences of our thoughts working through us. We must retrain our thoughts so that they do not continually frustrate God's plans, the amazing feats that He wants to accomplish through us. Because satan has sown so much negativity, we often encourage thoughts and desires that cannot possibly harmonize with the Spirit of God within. Did you know that God is a positive thinker? God thinks positively about all of His children because He can see past their present circumstances to the time when they will be just like Him. Because God has such great vision for the future, God is never discouraged by the trifling matters of the present. That means we do not have to be moved by our circumstances either. Instead we can think about them in the same fashion that God thinks about them. It goes right back to our godly imagination. Can we imagine ourselves free and full of joy? If we can, then it will not be long before we really are free and full of joy.

God shapes His circumstances and environment by the way He thinks. Good thoughts and actions can never produce bad results. Bad thoughts and actions can never produce good results. The only reason we get into so much trouble is because we don't know how to bridle our thoughts and direct them according to God's plan and purpose for our life. We can learn how to, however, by meditating on things that are of God; things that are pure, lovely, just, holy, and of good report. We may not have the ability to choose our circumstances at first, but we can choose the thoughts that will directly shape our circumstances. In the same way, we cannot choose the family we grew up in; but we can choose to forgive and forget and not allow past patterns of behavior from our families, generational curses and iniquities, to crop up and control the way we think and act today and into the future.

I have watched patterns of harmful thinking go around and around in my own family. People have said things like, "You are just like so and so." That statement can be powerful for the enemy. In stupid statements like that, the devil is trying to bring a mindset and plant a thought that will lock us into that character and cycle of life that that person went through. I tell people, do not lock yourself into a certain disposition or mindset. Prepare yourself for the move of God that He is going to bring forth through your life. Prepare yourself for what God wants to do through you. There are people reading this book right now that God wants to use to grow new arms and legs. He wants to translate you in the Spirit, and take you to foreign countries to minister the Gospel of Jesus Christ! God has got big plans for you!

If things like that have ever been spoken over you, prepare yourself for what God wants to do in you by allowing Him to cleanse your mind. God may want to do powerful miracles through you, but a negative mindset will stop God from moving in you.

A man only becomes a man when he ceases to grumble and complain, and decides to seek God's hidden justice, which regulates his life.

Grumbling and complaining never took the Israelites anywhere except in a circle for 40 years. We need to practice bridling thoughts of discontentedness and bitterness against what God is working in us and doing through us. Practice directing your thoughts toward God's massive plan and purpose for your life. Run the race to win the prize.

Make no mistake; God has big plans for you.

He is setting up big things for you to do.

By thinking God's thoughts, regardless of the circumstances that you are in now, you can shape your environment.

THE HEARING EAR

In Mark chapter 4, Jesus made a rather peculiar statement, "If anyone has ears to hear, let him hear." Now in all probability everyone in the crowd had physical ears to hear with. So what did he mean?

I think the ear He was speaking of had something to do with being ready to receive the revelation that only comes from the Spirit of God.

> *Be careful what you are hearing. The measure [of thought and study] that you give [to the truth that you hear] will be the measure [of virtue and knowledge] that comes back to you—and more [besides] will be given to you who hear* (Mark 4:24 AMP).

A lot of us hear the truth, but we just don't see the benefits of living out the Word. We don't apply it, or esteem it. We don't honor and respect the truth that we hear.

If we listen carefully to the Word of God by making it the subject of our thought life, we begin to adhere to it, honor it, respect it, and progressively apply it. Then, as the verse above states, it will come back to us in virtue and knowledge. I have experienced this many times in my own life. For example, Isaiah 58:6-8 says:

> *Is this not the fast that I have chosen: To loose the bonds of wickedness, to undo the heavy burdens, to let the oppressed go free, and that you break every yoke? Is it not to share your bread with the hungry, and that you bring to your house the poor who are cast out; when you see the naked, that you cover him, and not hide yourself from*

your own flesh? Then your light shall break forth like the morning, your healing shall spring forth speedily, and your righteousness shall go before you; the glory of the Lord shall be your rear guard.

Many times I have meditated on this Scripture. God revealed to me that if I fasted the way He wanted me to, I would experience divine health in my life like I had never experienced it before. God instructed me to go on a 40-day water fast. I did what I was instructed, and I felt better than I had ever felt before. Again the Lord told me to go on another 40-day water fast. So I did. Again, my health increased and my body became stronger. As I meditated on God's Word, His Word became actions in my life, and those actions brought the fruit of divine health. Finally God commanded me to go on a third 40-day fast which included juice. In the span of three years, I had gone on three forty day fasts. After the third fast, I had an incredible sense and assurance from the Lord that a new level of divine immunity had been reached. Knowing clearly by revelation that Jesus the healer lives in me and I believe this kind of meditation moves into my actions and brings a healed life into continual being. By revelation of the Word of God became flesh, I AM, God's healing is permanently residing in me. Since that third 40-day fast, I thank God I have not been sick one day. God's instructions to you may be different. He may have you meditate on a different Scripture and give you different instructions in order to see that revelatory Word become flesh in your life. As you meditate on the Word and are obedient to act out God's instructions, you will experience the fruit of obedience in your own life.

When we turn our ear to the truth, the truth will be implanted. When it is implanted it will be remembered.

The Holy Spirit is not bound to the same type of existence as we are currently experiencing. He is past, present, and future, all at the same time. He always brings all things to our remembrance and shows us things to come, because He is not limited to time or space. He is now. He knows the mind of God concerning the future and can bring forth the mind of God into the now.

Note the Spirit's role in the following passage:

> *But God has revealed them to us through His Spirit. For the Spirit searches all things, yes, the deep things of God. For what man knows the things of a man except the spirit of the man which is in him? Even so no one knows the things of God except the Spirit of God. Now we have received, not the spirit of the world, but the Spirit who is from God, that we might know the things that have been freely given to us by God.*
>
> *These things we also speak, not in words which man's wisdom teaches but which the Holy Spirit teaches, comparing spiritual things with spiritual. But the natural man does not receive the things of the Spirit of God, for they are foolishness to him; nor can he know them, because they are spiritually discerned. But he who is spiritual judges all things, yet he himself is rightly judged by no one. For "who has known the mind of the Lord that he may instruct Him?" But we have the mind of Christ* (1 Corinthians 2:10-16).

> *For who has known or understood the mind (the counsels and the purposes) of the Lord so as to guide and instruct Him and give Him knowledge? But we have the mind of Christ (the Messiah) and do hold the thoughts (feelings and purposes) of His heart* (1 Corinthians 2:16 AMP).

The mind of the Messiah is to hold the thoughts, feelings, and purposes of His heart. We should want this. We should want to hold the thoughts, feelings, and purposes of His heart. We should want to possess them.

The Holy Spirit can bring to mind anything that we need as a resource from the past, to bring forth the unction of God and the wisdom of God, so that we can convey the clear thoughts of God in the now.

We, like our Messiah, have an anointed mind. We have an anointing that abides in us and teaches us all things, the Scripture says. We have an unction from the Holy One, the Messiah, who knows all things (see 1 John 2:20). The word unction is a very unique word, whose Greek counterpart is only used three times in the New Covenant writings. *Charisma*, which literally means an unguent or a smearing of ointment or oil,[3] is also translated "anointing." It is metaphorical of the Holy Spirit indwelling a believer and enduing him or her with spiritual power. An unction, therefore, is an endowment of the Holy Spirit. This unction will bring all things to our remembrance, will reveal the truth in our present circumstances, and will show us things to come. The Holy Spirit knows the thoughts of the past, the thoughts of the present, and the thoughts of the future.

An anointed mind can understand, declare, administer, and speak forth the thoughts of the Spirit.

In truth, we have the actual mind of the Messiah, the Anointed One (*Christ* is a Greek translation of Messiah, which means "God's anointed one").[4] He is the Anointed One, because like the kings of the Old Covenant, He had been anointed with the oil of anointing—in the case of Jesus the anointing oil was the Holy Spirit. So if we have the mind of Christ, then we also have the mind of the Anointed One and are marked by God with His anointing. Every Spirit-filled believer has been anointed by the Holy Spirit and has the mind of Christ.

We have an anointed mind. It is an anointed mind because, just like our Messiah, we have been endued with power from on high. Because we have been anointed with the Holy Spirit, we are able to receive the things of the Spirit.

Jesus is our example, our goal. When Jesus spoke anointed words, they produced anointed results. The anointed results were the glory of God. In other words, it was the fruit of the anointing that was responsible for producing the glory.

When anointed thoughts are birthed into action,
we see the glory of God.

Today God is still birthing anointed thoughts in His people by the Word and the Holy Spirit. When anointed thoughts and ideas are birthed, they will lead to anointed words and actions. Then we will see the glory of God.

> *"If anyone has ears to hear, let him hear." Then He said to them, "Take heed what you hear. With the same measure you use, it will be measured to you; and to you who hear, more will be given* (Mark 4:23-24).

The words **take heed** are from the Greek word *blepo*, which means: (figuratively) to hold the mind, i.e. pay attention to, be cautious about, apply oneself to, adhere to: (give) attend (-ance, -ance at, -ance to, unto), beware, be given to, give (take) heed (to unto); have regard.[5]

The simple translation of "take heed what you hear" does not do the original words of this Scripture justice. We should know that **the amount of energy in our mind that we apply to retain something is what will come back to us**. In other words, we must pay attention closely to what we hear (from God), knowing that the amount of attention we give will come back to us.

> *When anointed words are spoken and received, anointed results will be produced.*

Sometimes we can hear a good message and walk away saying, "Yes, it was good preaching," but then we can't remember even one sentence that was preached. Somehow when the minister was preaching, our brains just weren't in gear. We did not receive clearly the thoughts of God concerning that message. It is possible for us to retain the Word of God however. It comes down to valuing what we are receiving. If we truly value the Word of God being preached, if we value the amount of time that the man or woman of God put into the Word he or she is sharing, we will take notes and go back and study what was said. When we do this, we are actually entering into the revelation that the mind of God in us has received from God. The anointed words the preacher is speaking will be able to take root in our hearts and produce the fruit of righteousness, peace, and joy in the Holy Spirit. In order for the truth to set us free, we must receive the truth. "You will *know* the truth, and the truth will make you free." Then the anointing that is on the man or woman of God will be able to flow through our lives because we have entered into what God is revealing to that person.

As the Rain Comes Down

"For My thoughts are not your thoughts,

Nor are your ways My ways," says the Lord.
"For as the heavens are higher than the earth,
So are My ways higher than your ways,
And My thoughts than your thoughts" (Isaiah 55:8-9).

Do not be mistaken; God is not saying that you cannot have His thoughts. If this were true, then the Lord would have never instructed Paul to write to the Corinthians, "We have the mind of Christ." God was telling Isaiah that he needs to make some adjustments in order to be able to get His thoughts. God is saying to Isaiah, "You have to adjust because I am not going to adjust. You have to change because of Me, in order for Me to get My thoughts across to you." God is making it clear to the Israelites that their natural way of thinking and doing things will never fit into God's big plan. His thoughts are high and cannot be brought low. His thoughts are original and carry creative power.

True, He first demonstrates how far away from Him we are: just like the heavens are higher than the earth. But soon the emphasis changes to how close we can get. In God's thinking, this distance is absolutely worthless. If we think about it correctly, having a huge gap between us and God does not help God out at all either. God created us to be in close, intimate, face-to-face fellowship with His person. If we are distanced from Him because of sin, fear, religion, etc. He will never be able to truly enjoy our company. We will never be able to fulfill the reason we were created in the first place. God is pointing out how utterly foolish it is for us to be constantly running away from His presence because it negates our reason for existing.

"Look how far away you are from Me. Now I will bring you to Me."

God does this with Job. He asks Job, "Can you hold the ocean in the palm of your hand? I weighed the universe in the balance. Where were you when I did that, Job?" (see Job 38:1-15).

In essence, He is saying to Job, "Don't try to insult my intelligence. Get in line with what I am thinking, Job." It took Job a while to change his own mindset. At first, even his wife told him to curse God and die. He went through a struggle for quite a while before he got his thought patterns corrected. God was showing Job that he could know what God knows and be where God is. Job did not have to remain distant and foreign to God. He did not have to live in fear of God's judgment. He could rise up to where God is if he just chose to. We have to get in line with God's way of thinking. God told Job that he had existed before the foundation of the earth was laid and that he ought to know what God was thinking about and doing from his first-hand experiences with God. God was saying to Job, "I'm the sovereign Creator, and you are My son. Now, walk and talk with Me where I am." It took Job a while to get his mindset adjusted, because he listened to the mixture that was coming out of the mouths of his friends. When He started listening to God exclusively, God brought the change to Job's thought patterns.

Again, in order to bridge the distance between our thoughts and the thoughts of God, we need to bridle our thoughts. In effect, we reject what the Spirit is trying to do when we just let our thoughts go everywhere. The Holy Spirit will lead us, but those earthly, sensual thoughts have to be bridled.

When a bit is placed in a horse's mouth, he doesn't like it. The bit in the mouth of the horse actually controls the tongue of the horse. When the bridle is pulled on, it causes the bit to put pressure on the tongue of the horse and causes the horse to go the direction that you want him to go. This is exactly the picture that James draws in chapter 3. James compares the tongue to the rudder of a ship. It is a very small part of the boat, but it has complete control over which direction the ship will go. In the same way, the tongue is the rudder of our lives. We will always head in the direction of our words. When the horse trainer puts the bit in the horse's mouth, the horse will be trained to move in the direction that the bit and the bridle lead him; he will no longer move in whatever direction he feels like going. If we put a bit in our mouths and a bridle on our minds, we will be trained to go in the direction that our trainer—the Holy Spirit—wants us to go. The bridle of our minds is the Word of God. The Word turns us in the direction that the Holy Spirit wants us to go. The bit is self-control. Because self-control helps us to speak only what we hear the Father speaking, it keeps words of worry, doubt, and discouragement from jumping into our thoughts and out of our mouths. We need to meditate on the Word so we know what direction God is taking us in, and we need to practice self-control by not allowing just anything to come shooting out of our mouths. We need to be very choosy about what we speak so that only what is of God is allowed to have voice.

Now use the remainder of this passage from Isaiah 55 to shed light on how God's thoughts function in the earth. Remember that God's Word naturally represents His way of thinking:

> *"For as the rain comes down,*
> [Put this in the context of God's thoughts]
> *and the snow from heaven,*
> *And do not return there,*
> *But water the earth,*
> [This is what I am doing with My thoughts. My thoughts influence the earth. My thoughts come down like rain.]
> *And make it bring forth and bud,*
> *That it may give seed to the sower*
> *And bread to the eater,*
> [This is speaking of the substance of God's thoughts. They are words that have been solidified. The words were birthed by thought.]
> *So shall My word be*
> [God's Word is a manifestation of His thoughts.]
> *that goes forth from My mouth;*
> [My thoughts that are spoken out]
> *It shall not return to Me void,*

But it shall accomplish what I please,
[because that is what I thought]
And it shall prosper in the thing for which I sent it.
[That is the fruitfulness of My thoughts.] (Isaiah 55:10-
11).

God's thoughts come to us like rain. But the rain comes down for
a purpose. It is meant to yield a crop.

I like the following quote from James Allen:

> Men imagine that thought can be kept secret, but it
> cannot. It rapidly crystallizes into habit and a habit
> solidifies into circumstances. Bestial thoughts crystal-
> lize into drunkenness and sensuality that solidify into
> circumstances of destruction and disease. Impure
> thoughts of every kind crystallize into enervating,
> confusing habits and solidify into distracting and
> adverse circumstances.[6]

Good or bad, our thoughts will produce. It's time we turn what
satan has for so long used for bad into something God intended for
good. Everything that exists in the universe was in the mind of God
before He ever created anything. God meditated on His plan and then
verbalized it. You were part of those thoughts! You were in existence
before the foundation of the earth was laid. Ephesians chapter 1, verse
4, tells us, "… just as He chose us in Him before the foundation of
the world, that we should be holy and without blame before Him in
love…." God thought good things, meditated on good, and so the
Word that He spoke was full of what is good. Therefore, when He
spoke, what came into being was good through and through. We have
the same ability that God has because He has given it to us. We can
think good thoughts; we can meditate on those good thoughts; we
can speak words that are full of what is good. The results will be that

God's goodness will be produced in our lives.

Isn't that the same principle demonstrated in the above verses?

Isn't that the purpose of the mind of Christ?

Let the thoughts of God produce fruit that will
bring you into a harvest.

We know from the Gospel of John chapter 1 that Christ is the Word made flesh. It stands to reason that having His mind is key to thinking like God. When we operate in the mind of Christ, an anointed mind, we are tapping into the power source that brought all things into existence and made the Word of God become flesh.

The rain came down.

God thought.

His thoughts, like rain, came down to the earth. The seeds that were sown turned into the plant that came forth and bore fruit. In this way, the Word did not return forth void. By penetrating our thoughts, it crystallized and turned into harvest. God wants to produce a God-sized harvest through us, His children. The Father wants to use us as conduits for His thoughts and Words. God wants us to operate in the imagination of Jesus Christ—an imagination that is not tainted by sin, perversity, and fear. God wants us to allow Him to put a bit in our mouths and bridle our minds so that we can be trained to think the thoughts of God and speak the Words of God.

By meditating day and night on God's Word, we will be continually focusing on what God thinks and says about everyday circumstances. We do not have to accept them the way they are. As children of God, we have the privilege and right to alter our circumstances by altering our thinking patterns about our circumstances.

Think Like God:
GOD-THOUGHTS FOR MEDITATION

- Christ-Consciousness is a pattern of behavior that centers on thinking anointed thoughts that create anointed words that produce anointed results.
- I declare that I think like my Father God. I declare that I talk like my Father God. I declare that I act like my Father God. I declare that the thoughts of God dominate me. I declare that the consciousness of God rules and reigns in me.
- Circumstances do not determine the outcome; your situation reveals your meditation.
- The thoughts you send out, you will receive back multiplied.
- A man becomes a man only when he ceases to grumble and complain, and decides to seek for God's hidden justice, which regulates his life.
- When we turn our ear to the truth, the truth will be implanted. When it is implanted it will be remembered.
- The Holy Spirit can bring to mind anything that we need as a resource from the past, to bring forth the unction of God and the wisdom of God, so that we can convey the clear thoughts of God in the now.
- An anointed mind can understand, declare, admin-

ister, and speak forth the thoughts of the Spirit.

- When anointed words are spoken and received, anointed results will be produced.
- Let the thoughts of God produce fruit that will bring you into a harvest.

ENDNOTES

1. James Strong. Strong's Exhaustive Concordance of the Bible: Greek Dictionary of the New Testament, (Nashville, TN: Thomas Nelson Publishers, 2001), 213.

2. http://www.watchtower.org/bible/joh/chapter_001.htm. Accessed 10/12/08.

3. James Strong. The New Strong's Expanded Exhaustive Concordance of the Bible: Strong's Expanded Greek Dictionary of the New Testament, (Nashville, TN: Thomas Nelson Publishers, 2001), 114-115.

4. Ibid., 213.

5. Ibid., 55.

6. James Allen. *As a Man Thinketh* (St. Augustine, FL: AsaManThinketh.net, 2001), 13.

Chapter Four

Walk in the Spirit

THE BREATH OF GOD

The NIV Bible states in Second Timothy 3:16 that every Scripture is God-breathed. I love this expression because it perfectly describes God's Word. To get a better picture of what this means, take a deep breath, and read or recite your favorite Bible verse. As you speak the words of the verse, what happens to the air that is in your lungs? It is slowly being released out of your mouth. We all know that when we take in a breath of air, our body takes the good things from the air, such as oxygen, to benefit the body. But did you know that when you breathe the air back out, there is still usable oxygen in the air? It is true! Scientifically speaking, there is just enough oxygen in the air that each person breathes out of his or her mouth to sustain life[1] in another body. You see, the body needs a calculated amount of oxygen in order to function. If it does not receive it, the body will die. Each time we breathe in our bodies are actually receiving much more oxygen than they can use. That is why people can give mouth-to-mouth resuscitation to another person if he or she has stopped breathing. We can actually breathe life-giving breath into another person's lungs and help them to live!

There is a great revelation to be learned by observing how God created our bodies to function. In many ways, our physical bodies demonstrate how we are truly image-bearers of God. When God created the man, Genesis says that He breathed the breath of life into him, and the man became a speaking spirit. It is interesting that the Hebrew word for spirit, *ruach*[2] (which is the word used in Genesis chapter 2, verse 7), is also translated as breath hundreds of times in the Hebrew Scriptures. God's breath of life and His life-giving Spirit are almost identical in meaning in many places in the Hebrew Scriptures. This shows us how God's Word is in partnership with God's Spirit. They are inseparable. This provides us with an excellent comparison. In the natural, if one cannot breathe, then one cannot speak. In the supernatural, without the breath (or Spirit) of God, God would not be able to speak His Word, nor would we have the ability to verbalize God's thoughts. God' breath, on which His Word is carried, has actually become a life-giving Spirit, according to First Corinthians 15:45. God's Word is infused with His life-giving breath. We should continually grow in our understanding of how God's Word is unparalleled in power because it is infused with the omnipotence of His Spirit. The Spirit of God and the Word of God are in perfect partnership to bring forth what God desires. (To learn more about the working relationship between the Spirit of God and the Word of God, please read author's book, *God Working With God!*)

> *"As for Me," says the Lord, "this is My covenant with them: My Spirit who is upon you, and My words which I have put in your mouth, shall not depart from your mouth, nor from the mouth of your descendents, nor from the mouth of your descendents' descendents," says the Lord, "from this time and forevermore"* (Isaiah 59:21).

God's Word is birthed out of the meditations of God's heart. Clearly all of God's Words were constantly being thought before they were ever spoken. His thoughts precede His Word in the same way that our thoughts precede our words. With everything that exists, everything God created in the earth, He thought about it first, before He verbalized it. He thought about it and He breathed. This makes obvious God's great self-control. God did not blurt out His Word until the correct time set in place by Himself to bring His meditations to fulfillment.

When He breathed He propelled His Words.

His thoughts were propitiated by His Words.

His life-giving breath propelled what He was thinking.

Jesus was relating this same concept when he stated, "I can speak nothing but what I hear My Father say." Do you suppose that He literally was *unable* to speak anything but what the Father said? Or did He mean, if He was to carry out His assignment with success (fulfilling the thoughts and plans of God), then He refused to speak anything but what the Spirit was empowering Him to speak. If He had an unbridled mind where He meditated on whatever popped up before Him, His words would have been unruly and unfruitful, as many of ours are. Not so, however, with Jesus. He practiced perfect discipline in the area of His thought life and words. He was the mouthpiece of His Father. In this way He was unable to speak anything but God's Words. He was constrained by the love of God and the mind of Christ.

Empowered as He was by the same Spirit (or breath) as His Father in Heaven was, He conveyed the thoughts of God through His words to the same exact degree of accuracy and power as His heavenly Father. He was filled with the Spirit of God, and the Spirit of God that was upon Him propelled the Words of God. Jesus brought forth the Word of God (*logos*), He allowed the Spirit of God to breathe on that Word so that it became the living Word (*rhema),* brought forth in power and in the demonstration of signs, wonders, and miracles. Through the Word of God become flesh, namely, Jesus, God sent His Word, which is the manifestation of His thoughts and meditation. This is what God has destined for us as His children: that the Word of God should become flesh in us and that His thoughts might manifest through us in signs, wonders, and miracles. Mark chapter 16, verses 16 through 18, says, "He who believes and is baptized will be saved; but he who does not believe will be condemned. And these signs will follow those who believe: In My name they will cast out demons; they will speak with new tongues; they will take up serpents; and if they drink anything deadly, it will by no means hurt them; they will lay hands on the sick, and they will recover." God has called all believers to signs and wonders, to heal the sick, raise the dead, and change the world. The way that we will accomplish these things is by allowing the Word of God to first change the way we think, and then change the way we act.

He Chose Us

In the same way that God meditated on creating the earth and all the plants and animals, God thought about each of us prior to our ever being born on this earth. He knew (which means to be intimately acquainted with) us before we were conceived. God meditated continually on us becoming just like Him. He thought about how we would demonstrate the power of His Word and bring His Kingdom to pass on the earth. He meditated on our victory, which was won for us at the Cross. That is why He could say with confidence in Isaiah 61, verse 4, **"And they shall rebuild the old ruins, they shall raise up the former desolations, and they shall repair the ruined cities, the desolations of many generations,"** and in verse 7, **"Instead of your shame you shall have double honor, and instead of confusion they shall rejoice in their portion. Therefore in their land they shall possess double; everlasting joy shall be theirs."** God could see past all the sin and failures of His children because He meditated on His own ability to bring them into victory and power!

Just as He chose us in Him before the foundation of the

world, that we should be holy and without blame before Him in love . . . (Ephesians 1:4).

God thought about us before the foundation of the world. Moreover, His thoughts were only of good. He chose us to be holy and blameless in His sight.

In the following verse, you can see God's *forethought.* God originally called you out of His Word. Your origin is in God, not in the broken down, sinful human nature! He spoke you and formed you out of the substance of His Word, and He is bringing you back to where you were drawn out of. God has a vision concerning your life, and He can see where He is bringing us from and where He is taking us to.

Then the word of the Lord came to me, saying:
"Before I formed you in the womb I knew you;
Before you were born I sanctified you;
I ordained you a prophet to the nations" (Jeremiah 1:4-5).

The word *to know* in the Hebrew is *yada.*[3] It has a very powerful meaning, because it does not just pertain to mind knowledge. According to *Strong's Dictionary*, it can mean to be intimately acquainted with, even in a sexual manner, such as when Adam "knew" his wife Eve, and she conceived (Genesis 4:1). *Yada* means to know in an intimate and personal way. In the above verse, the verb *to know* is paralleled with the verb *to sanctify.* In the Hebrew Scriptures, parallels are used to imply equality or an intertwining relationship between the two statements. This form of writing is used quite often in the Psalms and Proverbs to show association between two actions. In this verse, God is relating the knowledge, intimate acquaintance, between God and Jeremiah to the prophet's sanctification and revelation.

According to *Strong's Exhaustive Concordance of the Bible,* this same connection can be seen in the revelation of God's name to

Moses, and His fulfillment of the promise to the children of Israel, which had been given to Abraham over 450 years earlier.[4] The fulfillment of the Promise, which was to receive the Promised Land, did not take place until God revealed Himself by His personal name, YHWH. The revelation or personal knowledge of God's name would have created a doorway for the people of Israel to receive the promise of God. Though Abraham, Isaac, and Jacob all worshiped God, they were not intimately acquainted with God's personal name.

The intimacy of knowing God in a personal and experiential way is key to coming into the fullness of what God has called us to be and do. "Knowing" God in an intimate way is imperative to receiving all that God has for us. We need to understand that before time began God was intimately acquainted with us; He loved us, sanctified us, called us, chose us, thought of us, spoke of us. Our origin is in God and His Word, and intimacy with God, a face-to-face encounter with the Truth, is what is going to set us free to become God's will in the earth.

At the time that the Lord spoke to Jeremiah, according to historians, the weeping prophet was only 8 years old. Notice, however, that God did not say to Jeremiah, "All right, kid, I know you're just a boy and you don't even know how to really speak yet. Somehow, I'm going to make you into a prophet. I know you don't look like much, and I'm as nervous about it as you are, but we'll make it work somehow!" God proclaimed to Jeremiah, "What I see in you is what you really are! What I have meditated on is going to be the reality that you see. I know who you are, Jeremiah. You are a prophet to the nations. Don't worry about what others think, because My thoughts toward you are for success and not failure. And My thoughts have never failed yet!" These verses tell me that God had a thought, because the word chosen means to make a volitional decision, to meditate upon, to think about inside. God knew that Jeremiah's true origin was in the mind of Christ, where God had been meditating on what He would do with this young man. Jeremiah proceeded out of God's thoughts![5]

Let God's written Word take on a prophetic voice in your life. God is speaking these verses over your life right now! God already knew beforehand where we would come from. He knew our gifts and calling before we were conceived in the womb. It does not matter the circumstances of our conception in the natural. It is completely irrelevant whether or not our natural parents chose us. God knew all that.

There are no spiritual accidents with God. This is because choice involves the power of thought. In order to choose, you have to think about it. After you consider something, then you make a volitional decision based upon what you have been thinking about. Like God, we make a decision based upon what we have been thinking about. The Bible says that we have been chosen in Him, in God, before God even made the earth.

GOD'S THOUGHTS TOWARD US ARE LOVE

To walk in the Spirit is to walk in and be ruled by the love of God. God is love. His love has been made obvious in the fact that He has already predestined for us to be conformed in His image and likeness. When we fell and sinned, He made a plan for atonement in His thoughts to restore us and bring us back into rightful unity and oneness with Him. He had the plan for us to be brought into the place of restoration with Him. God knows what is best for us. The Bible even teaches that God is very slow to anger and quick to show mercy and forgiveness. Seven times in the Old Covenant Scriptures, it tells us that God is slow to anger. Joel chapter two, verse 13, tells us, "So rend your heart, and not your garments; Return to the LORD your God, For He is gracious and merciful, **Slow** to **anger**, and of great kindness; And He relents from doing harm." He does not meditate on our past failures or hold a grudge against us for not following through with the commands He gave us. Even though these things disappoint God, He never dwells on the past. His love has the ability to change the past. Love has the power to transform our thoughts from thoughts of unforgiveness and bitterness to mercy and forgiveness. Love changes our meditations about people who have hurt us in the past and gives us the ability to forgive and forget, just as God has done for us. When we walk in humility toward God, it will be easy to see that it was love for the Father and love for us that nailed Jesus to the Cross. Jesus told His disciples, "Greater love has no man than this: that he lays down his life for his friends." Jesus made the greatest sacrifice in order to manifest God's love. We must choose to do the same.

Think about Jesus on the Cross. Even though the soldiers had beat Him and spit on Him, reviling Him and calling Him names, He said to the Father, "Forgive them, for they do not know what they are doing." He meditated on thoughts of love and forgiveness, and because of this, the centurion who watched Him die actually came to know that He was the Son of God. "Truly," he said, "this man was the Son of God (Matthew 27:54)." Our thoughts of love toward another person can even break down walls between them and God, so that they come to the saving knowledge of Jesus Christ.

Our thoughts involve what we believe.

People always meditate on what they believe deep down in their hearts. They may even claim to believe something completely different than what is truly in their hearts; however, their minds are much less deceptive than their mouths, when it comes to sticking to what they really believe. The Scripture says that the words of these people are smoother than honey, but make the stomach bitter. Unfortunately the mind is where the real deception lies: these people are convinced that what *they* believe about themselves is *really truth*. This is a concept that my wife Kayla calls blind conceit. It is our pride that blinds us from seeing the truth about ourselves and others. David prayed that the Lord would set him free from blind conceit. When we choose to fashion our view of ourselves according to our own perceptions we are allowing our conceit to blind us. If I draw a picture of an animal that has never been seen before, I am the one who decides what it looks like. The animal has no choice as to what it will turn out to be, because I am the creator of it. It will be what I want it to be. This is true about us also. Even if we pretend to be one thing, unless we are being what God says about us, we are not really being *who and what we truly are!* In order to know ourselves, we must give into what God has said we will be. We need to choose to believe and meditate on what God thinks about us. We need to formulate our very existence around His thoughts toward us. His thoughts toward us are full of good. We really have nothing to be afraid of.

We see repeatedly in Scripture that God chose us before the foundations of the world; in the Hebrew Scriptures, God set the nation of Israel apart and told them to come out from among those who do not know Him. In the New Covenant, we are instructed to be in the world, but not of the world (see Romans 12:1-2), showing through our words and actions that we are set apart, holy, and chosen. Paul tells us in Ephesians chapter 1 that God chose us in Him before the foundation of the world, that we should be holy and without blame before Him in love. This verse reveals that God was meditating on thoughts of love concerning us long before the world was formed. He wasn't only thinking of Jeremiah—God thought about us too. The Bible teaches us that God (Love) is no respecter of persons. Yet we can see from the Word that God is a respecter of Himself. The Lord is not interested in thoughts of the flesh or thoughts that come from the enemy; He is only interested in what has been birthed from His Spirit. As God has called all to repentance, we can see that God's love is for everyone, just as His power, His mind, and His thoughts are for everyone. God makes His thoughts available to anyone who will receive them.

He came to His own, and His own did not receive Him.
But as many as received Him, to them He gave the right

to become children of God, to those who believe on His
name: who were born, not of blood, nor of the will of the
flesh, nor of the will of man, but of God (John 1:11-13).

Before God created the earth He picked us out. We are fearfully
and wonderfully made. God knew where we would be today. He
knew us and chose us before the foundations of the world!

THOUGHTS OF A SON

God thought about sending His only Son to save us. He knew
what the price of sending His Son would be. He meditated on His
love for us so much that He was willing to sow His own life to reap a
harvest of many lives. In the same way, Abraham became convinced
of the bigness of God when He meditated on the stars. He knew when
the Lord came to him and commanded him to sacrifice his only son
whom he loved, namely Isaac, that God was able to raise Isaac from
the dead. Abraham knew the cost of love. Abraham knew that God
wanted devotion that would give up the thing most precious to him.
If Abraham had not meditated on God's bigness, he would have never
been able to imagine God raising his son Isaac from the dead. In his
thought life, however, Abraham was convinced of God's power and
faithfulness. Hebrews chapter 11, verses 17, 18, and 19, says:

> *By faith Abraham, when he was tested, offered up Isaac,*
> *and he who had received the promises offered up his only*
> *begotten son, of whom it was said, "In Isaac your seed*
> *shall be called," concluding that God was able to raise*
> *him up, even from the dead, from which he also received*
> *him in a figurative sense.*

Abraham was able to see what God was saying concerning his son
Isaac. God had promised to bring forth a great nation from Isaac. In

his inner imagination, Abraham received Isaac raised from the dead because he could see the bigness of God working in his own life. He knew already the bigness of God had been manifested in his life by the birth of a son from a barren womb and a man who was already 100 years old (see Genesis 21:5). Therefore, he was willing to give up Isaac, believing all along that true devotion to God would bring a harvest.

Thought strongholds of fear, lack, doubt, unbelief, sickness, and death are not God's thoughts.

In the same way God meditated on sowing His only begotten Son. God knew in His thoughts that Jesus would have to die on the Cross and shed His blood to forgive us for our sins and cleanse us from all unrighteousness before He ever carried any action out. He knew that His one and only Son would be the firstborn among many other sons and daughters to come.

For God so loved the world, that He gave His only begotten Son, that whoever believes in Him should not perish but have everlasting life (John 3:16).

Within God's love sacrifice we see the principle of sowing and reaping. God sowed a God-seed in order to reap a God-harvest (read *God Working With God*). What does this mean? It means that God sowed His only Son in order to reap a harvest of millions of sons! Remember, as a man thinks in his heart, so is he. That same principle applies to God. God is abundant (just take a look at His universe); therefore, His thoughts are of abundance. The same principle of seed time and harvest that God put into the earth at the beginning of time applied to God all along, because the principle itself is part of God's nature and character. God created the earth to be plentiful and full of harvest. He created the land to produce, to take a few seeds and make a whole field of ripe plants, each carrying hundreds of seeds. It is part of God's nature to produce something colossal from something very small. God's thoughts toward us are abundant thoughts of more than enough and overflowing favor and goodness.

Every one of God's Words in the Bible reveals the plentiful and bountiful thoughts of God. They reveal to us the mind of God. That is why He said if you meditate upon My Words day and night that it will be health to your flesh.

> *My son, give attention to My words;*
> *Incline your ear to My sayings.*
> *Do not let them depart from your eyes,*
> *Keep them in the midst of your heart:*
> *for they are life to those who find them,*
> *And health to all their flesh* (Proverbs 4:20-22).

Everything that God created, including our bodies, is subject to the Word of God. If we see something in our natural lives that does not line up with what God says, we should begin to speak the Word of God over that situation. Remember what John 1:11-13 teaches us: we are not born of the flesh, nor are we ruled by the flesh. We are born of God. We are born of the Spirit of Life! When a man becomes a Christian, he trades in his natural genes (those things which dictate who and what that man will become) for the genes of God. He now has God's DNA, His life pattern, and the man's spiritual and physical composition will now be fashioned after the Lord's pattern. Christians must realize what they have received when they became born of the Spirit. Within God's genes there is no death, fear, worry, sickness, disease, that can hold Him! Jesus was and is perfect in Spirit, soul, and body; in whose image we have been fashioned after. We are in covenant with an immortal, resurrected man.

When, over many years, people think like the world thinks, they have established many thoughts that have caused strongholds to come into their minds that should never have been there in the first place. These strongholds are contrary to the things above.

God is Love. Love had a love-thought that developed into a love plan, which was proclaimed in words wrapped with the nature of Love: Love's design was to bring love to completion by redeeming His vessels of love and transforming them into the nature and fullness of Love.

We need to think like we are children of God. Part of walking in the Spirit is allowing our thoughts to be focused on furthering the Kingdom of God at all times. We have to have Kingdom thoughts. If we don't get our thought life lined up with God, then deception will come in and deceive us. We have to think like Jesus thought. Do you know that Jesus meditated on joy? Hebrews chapter 12 says, "For the joy that was set before Him, He endured the cross." Jesus set the joy of who He was before His eyes day and night. Jesus meditated on what God thought about Him all the time. That is why He could say with confidence, "The Father loves the Son and has given Him all things." Jesus let God's thoughts about Him captivate His thinking. The joy of pleasing the Father is what created endurance in Jesus to walk through very difficult circumstances.

Selfish thoughts will produce selfishness; bitter thoughts will produce bitterness; Kingdom thoughts will produce souls. In this manner, the Kingdom of God has come and it is within us. God wants to birth the Kingdom of God from within us, starting with our thinking patterns.

Jesus is the Lamb slain before the foundation of the world. He knew that a seed had to be planted. He knew that the seed had to die. God sowed a seed wrapped with His love; He reaped millions of sons and daughters because of it. God sowed a seed of perfection; He is looking for a harvest of perfection. God sowed a seed of purity; He is looking for a harvest of purity. God sowed a seed of passion; He is looking for a harvest of passion—people who are driven by the fire of desire, to be intimately acquainted with Jesus. God sowed an incorruptible, immortal, omnipotent seed. He is expecting to reap a harvest that is incorruptible, immortal, and omnipotent. These are the meditations of God toward you. God thinks of us as incorruptible, immortal, and omnipotent. He thinks of you as perfect, pure, and passionate. If He did not think of you this way, He would be denying the principle of seed time and harvest that He set into place before the foundation of the world was laid.

> *Whoever abides in Him does not sin. Whoever sins has neither seen Him nor known Him.... Whoever has been born of God does not sin, for His seed remains in him; and he cannot sin, because he has been born of God* (1 John 3:6,9).

God wanted children, so He knew he had to sow a Son. He knew that He had to send a Son and thereby plant a seed. When we accept the death and resurrection of that seed, then we become a part of that process. Just as a seed falls into the ground and dies in order to produce more seed, so Christ died and was raised to life, to reap the harvest of many sons and daughters. We have been baptized into Christ (Messiah). We have literally put on Christ. We have become one with Him in the fellowship of His sufferings and the power of His resurrection. We have been made equal in Christ's death and in His resurrection.

Now do you see how the Kingdom of God has come and is within you? The Spirit is constantly telling us we are seated in heavenly places. The Spirit is constantly telling us that we are joint heirs with Christ. *After all, we do have His Word on that, do we not?*

When we minister or witness to others, we do it from the Spirit realm and from the Kingdom of God. The Kingdom of God has come within us. But for that concept to be fully realized, we have to minister from the consciousness of Christ in us. We have to minister from the position of being ambassadors and a chosen generation, the Ecclesia of God. *Ecclesia* is the Greek word translated as "church" in the English Bible, but it actually means the "called out ones." We need to think of ourselves as called out, set apart, fully equipped, soldiers of the heavenly Kingdom, enforcing the mass takeover of God's power on the earth.

When you have truly been born again, the real you does not sin.

There is a calling on all of our lives. It is in the Spirit. We have been seated in heavenly places. That means that we are *in the Spirit.* From now on when we see the word *heaven* we should not see it as something in the distance. We should see it as something that is right here with us. The Kingdom of Heaven has come and has won the final battle against the kingdom of darkness. Now the only question is, are we as His ambassadors going to go out and enforce our right to rule? This is the attitude that Jesus had in everything He did and said. He knew His position as the Son of God was to have dominion. He knew that it was His right and privilege to make all things in Heaven and all things on earth one in Christ.

Your Kingdom come, Your will be done in earth as it is in heaven.

Let what the Spirit wants to do in the natural have full rule and reign in you. Let the Holy Spirit have His freedom and the full expression of His ability in the natural just as He would in the spirit.

How do we begin this? We need to think like we are children of God. We have to train ourselves to think like Jesus thought. When Jesus saw a blind person, He thought, "My Father hates blindness. My Father wants us to see clearly." Then Jesus would lay hands on that person, and he would see. When Jesus saw a lame person, He thought, "My Father wants this man to walk and not grow weary, to run and not faint. In order to do that, He needs new legs!" Then, He would command the man to walk. When Jesus saw a barrier or a hindrance in the natural, He would meditate on the solution in the Spirit realm. After He thought about it, He would speak it. This was His normal pattern of behavior. We have to train ourselves to respond the way Jesus would respond if He were there in our stead. For, in fact, we are dead and our lives are hidden with Christ in God. Jesus is the one in us willing and doing what Jesus would do. Jesus was the Son, the First born. We are His brothers and sisters. We must train ourselves to think like sons and daughters. A good example of this happened in my own life while I was preaching in South Africa in a Portuguese ministers conference. When I was finished preaching, I was sitting on the stage. I opened my Bible to Isaiah 45:11. The verse says, "***Thus says the Lord, the Holy One of Israel and his Maker: Ask Me of things to come concerning My sons; and concerning the work of My hands ,you command Me.***" As I was meditating on this, I asked the Lord, "Who can command you?" The truth took on flesh as God revealed to me the rights, privileges, and directives that are available as a son of God. When we remind God of His Promises in His Word, it is like a command to God because He keeps His Word (commands). At this point the revelation of being a son absolutely exploded in my spirit. Before my eyes in the natural I saw a paralyzed woman in a wheelchair on the front row, and without any hesitation, I jumped off the stage and yelled at the top of my lungs, "I AM a son of God!" as I grabbed the woman by the hand, who by the way was extremely startled, and pulled her out of the wheelchair. Immediately strength came to her legs and she started to walk and run. She told me later, "I didn't really even have faith to be healed. I didn't expect anyone to pray for me." You see, it did not necessarily have to do with the woman's faith. It had to do with the fact that I recognized in my mind who I truly was and stepped out manifesting sonship.

Let the will of God in the Spirit realm be the will of God in the natural realm.

In fact, I believe it is impossible to keep our thoughts in the Spirit, or for that matter be successful in the Spirit realm, without developing our minds to be more aware of the fact that we are God's children. Unless we are thinking like God's children we will never be able to accomplish the greater works that our older Brother Jesus said we can do.

FAITH AND LOVE

Both faith and love are intimately connected to a person's thought life. Faith is developed in people's thoughts. What do they think about God's Word? Do they believe God's Word is true? Do they listen to others who love God and His Word, or do they listen to people full of doubt and confusion? What do they meditate on? Do they watch movies with death and sickness pervading them, or do they meditate on healing the sick, cleansing the leper, and raising the dead? What is their focus? We should ask ourselves these questions. How we answer them will show us where we are in faith. Faith comes from meditating on what God wants to do and will do if we just believe. Remember, the Scripture says, all things are possible to him who believes (see Mark 9:23). Am I thinking about things that will strengthen my belief that God's Word is true or am I listening to the voice of reason that says what I see in the natural is true, whether it lines up with God's Word or not? Faith starts with how we choose to think about God and His Word.

In the same fashion, Love begins with our thoughts. Love is an unlimited power source that is released first through our thoughts. If we come under attack from another person, it is possible to silence spiritual warfare by releasing thoughts of love and forgiveness.

Faith starts when we stop arguing with God.

Love starts with how we choose to think about another person. We might have an irritation with a person who goes to church with us. We may even have the desire to grumble and complain about that person. We have to realize that grumbling and complaining, gossip and slander all start in the thought life. Part of loving another person is thinking about them the way that God thinks about them. We have to stop operating in a critical and judgmental spirit, and start releasing God's love. When we release God's love, it will cause people's lives to be transformed, instead of hindering their growth in the spirit by thinking unholy thoughts about them. Love has the power to set others free.

We have to realize that here is an anointing that dwells in our hearts. (The heart is speaking of the center or the core of our consciousness. It's really the center of our being: who we really are.) We have been anointed with the Holy Spirit and with fire. We have an anointed mind—the mind of Christ. There is an anointing that dwells in our hearts because the Scripture says that Christ will dwell in our hearts through faith that is rooted and grounded in love. We must recognize that the anointing will flow through us only to the degree that the love of God is manifesting in our lives. Christ, the Anointed One and His anointing, are rooted and grounded in love.

That Christ may dwell in your hearts through faith; that you, being rooted and grounded in love, may be able to comprehend with all the saints what is the width and

length and depth and height—to know the love of Christ
which passes knowledge; that you may be filled with all
the fullness of God.

Now to Him who is able to do exceedingly abundantly
above all that we ask or think, according to the power
that works in us, to Him be glory in the church by Christ
Jesus to all generations, forever and ever. Amen
(Ephesians 3:17-21).

Faith is the substance of things hoped for and the evidence of
things not seen (see Hebrews 11:1). Faith must be rooted and
grounded in love. Faith is energized by love. When we accept the position that God has given us, a position of favor and love, our faith will
be propelled forward by the truth of God's goodness toward us. Our
faith is energized when we begin to think like a child of God.

When we walk out the nature of love, it silences
spiritual warfare.

Love has unique and unlimited power. As it takes operation in
our thoughts, it will begin to unveil things. Love has the power to
unlock revelation in our spirits. It turns a light bulb on in the
unknown darkness. It changes the way we think and view situations
in life. A lack of love can hinder true faith from operating through us.

Having faith that is rooted and grounded in love starts with how
we think. When we truly operate in love, it will open doors of utterance in another person's life so that we can minister to them. Love
will give us access to the mind of Christ concerning the word of
knowledge, word of wisdom, and discerning of spirits. Love will
uncover what is not of God in another person in order to transform
them. This kind of love begins with how we think about people.
Love is the opposite of sin, because if we truly love God, we keep

His commandments. Love offers a solution to difficult situations, because love has eyes to see past hindrances in the natural. God's power is birthed out of a "love mentality."

The power of faith can only be unleashed in and through a person who is constrained by the love of Christ.

Personally, I have experienced how love can open a person's eyes to see what has been placed in another person by God. My wife and I have been married 17 years, and the longer we are married the more we love one another. When my wife and I are together, she knows exactly what I am thinking and what I am going through. She knows where God is taking me, because she sees me through the eyes of love. She knows my God-designed destiny and believes in the God in me. She will look at me and know exactly why I say and do certain things. Then she will minister to me out of Love's recourses. She has taught me much about the power of Love just by loving me every day.

Miracles are a result of continual meditation on God's love. If we compare faith and love to a jet plane, Faith is what the jet plane was created to do. The jet plane says, "I was born to fly. I was fashioned to soar. I was created to break the sound barrier." However, if that plane has no jet fuel, it will never leave the runway. Love is the jet fuel for our plane. Faith says, "This blind man was made to see." Love says, "God wants him to see *NOW!*" Faith says, "My God shall supply all my *needs*." Love says, "My God gives me access to *overflow*—pressed down, shaken together, and running over. I will lend to many and borrow from none!" Faith is a belief that God is omnipotent. Love is a demonstration of God's omnipotence through signs and wonders. Faith that works by love starts with what we meditate on, what we think about God, ourselves, and other people.

Faith is the desire to do the impossible. Faith says, "Let's get a move on! Let's make something happen!" For example, at times when

I am ministering, faith will rise up and the Spirit will urge me to say, "Lady, step out in the aisle, God showed me you need healing." When they step out in the aisle, faith gets excited because it is rooted and grounded in love. Faith says, "God wants to heal you," and love says, "I see you are having lower back pain. Be healed in Jesus' name!" The anointing is then released through the channel of God's love, and the person is healed! This all starts with our thoughts. Do I spend time meditating every day on God's bigness and what the Word says about healing, or do I spend my time meditating on my circumstances and forget about what God says? When I meet someone who needs to be touched by the power of God, will my mind be full of God's love for that person or not? That depends on what I am thinking about.

The combined operation of faith that works by love begins in the thoughts.

The minute that we get sick, the first thought we have should not be to take a pill or go to see a doctor. That is how the world naturally thinks because that is all they have. They are surrounded by death and sickness, so their thoughts are full of it. If we surround ourselves with life, our minds will be full of life, not death!

THOUGHT LIFE AND PURITY

The way to truly surround ourselves with life is to renew our mind in the Word of God. The first thought that we need to have with any attack of the enemy is a reaction that is birthed out of the thoughts of God. When we remember that there is no weapon formed against us that will prosper and every tongue that rises against us in judgment shall be condemned (see Isaiah 54:17), it affects our thoughts and our actions. We have to meditate on what the Word of God says about us instead of what the enemy is trying to convince us is true, even though it is not true! We need to get the mind of God so that we can think more like God in everyday circumstances. At first, this may be difficult, because you are breaking old patterns of thinking that have been part of your life for a long time. But as you practice casting down thoughts that you know do not line up with the Word, and as you replace them with the thoughts of God, this process of recognizing thought strongholds and tearing them down will become easier. Recall what Jesus said when the devil came to him to tempt Him in the wilderness, "It is written...." That is another way of saying, "God's thoughts on this situation are as follows...."

And when it comes to God's thoughts in relationship to us, we can always have faith for the best. What God has in mind for us is better than our biggest imagination!

> *Finally, brethren, whatever things are true, whatever things are noble, whatever things are just, whatever things are pure, whatever things are lovely, whatever things are of good report, if there is any virtue and if there is anything praiseworthy—meditate on these things* (Philippians 4:8).

Whatever is worthy of reverence and honorable and seemly, whatever is just, whatever is pure, whatever is lovely and lovable, whatever is kind and winsome and gracious, if there is any virtue and excellence, if there is anything worthy of praise, fix your mind on them. Get your thoughts geared in the right direction—in the direction of God's glory and goodness. Thinking on these things will open your heart and your spirit to receive what God wants to share with you. When you think these thoughts, you will begin to get the mind of God and God will be with you. In this way you will function in the Spirit. When the meditations of our hearts are pure, and then we enter the realm of the Spirit to minister to other people, divine clarity and focus will come.

It is important to get our hearts and minds in the purity and holiness of the Spirit of God. In the Book of Matthew chapter 5, verse 8, Jesus states that it is the pure in heart who will see God. Psalm 24 also says that he who has clean hands and a *pure heart* can dwell in the mountain of the Lord. Having a *pure heart* has to do with what we think about on a consistent basis.

Purity creates clarity. Clarity creates a voice in the Spirit. A voice in the Spirit creates a doorway of utterance. A doorway of utterance creates a breakthrough.

Purity is, of course, in both the thought realm and the realm of your actions. Why do you think Jesus had such a stern warning against those that committed sins in their heart? He gave this warning because actions are birthed out of what we think about. For example, let us say that I have been sitting in the office all day. Since early this morning, however, I have been thinking about the steak my wife said she was going to make for dinner this evening. I am meditating on that steak! I can almost taste it, so juicy and with just the right spices. My mouth is watering! By the time I walk out of that office, I am ready for that steak. It would be pretty ridiculous then for me to go home and tell my wife, "I don't want any steak tonight, Honey. I'll just have a salad." That would not line up with my thoughts. I would be going against everything I have been thinking all day! This is how sin gets a hold of us without us even realizing it. Satan begins to bring thoughts into our heads. At the beginning they may seem harmless; I promise you, however, that the little thoughts lead to big thoughts. Little thoughts of doubt and confusion can lead to big thoughts of rebellion and rejection! Soon, we are not only thinking those thoughts, we are also speaking them. Then our actions and reactions to people are based on what we have been thinking. Purity toward God and toward others starts with our thoughts.

When we realize we are His children, we are energized by faith and learn to walk in love. Remember, with knowledge comes responsibility. The more revelation we get on being His children, the higher the call to purity. As we grow in the knowledge of God, the Father expects us to grow in walking out His purity in the Spirit. When our thoughts and deeds are pure, as we enter the realms of the Spirit, clarity will come.

> *How great is the love the Father has lavished on us that we should be called children of God! And that is what we are! The reason the world does not know us is that it did not know him. Dear friends, now we are children of God, and what we will be has not yet been made known. But we know that when He appears, we shall be like Him, for we shall see Him as He is. Everyone who has this hope in him purifies himself, just as He is pure* (1 John 3:1-3 NIV).

Becoming like Him starts now. When you purify yourself and start getting rid of old thought patterns and ways of behaving, the things of God will become clear to you. Thinking God's thoughts will break barriers in your life that you never thought possible. Remember, you were chosen before the foundation of the Earth was laid. God meditated on you before He ever created you with His Word. His thoughts toward you are love. This means that you can truly walk out the love of God toward God, toward yourself, and toward others, starting in the way that you think. Meditating on the purity and holiness of God helps to keep your thoughts in line with God's way of thinking and doing things. God's glory is increasing in your thoughts every second!

Think Like God
GOD-THOUGHTS FOR MEDITATION

- Our thoughts involve what we believe.
- Thought strongholds of fear, lack, doubt, unbelief, sickness, and death are not God's thoughts.
- God is Love. Love had a love-thought that developed into a love plan, which was proclaimed in words wrapped with the nature of Love: Love's design was to bring love to completion by redeeming His vessels of love and transforming them into the nature and fullness of Love.
- When you've truly been born again, the real you does not sin.
- Let the will of God in the Spirit realm be the will of God in the natural realm.
- Faith starts when we stop arguing with God.
- When we walk out the nature of love, it silences spiritual warfare.
- The power of faith can only be unleashed in and through a person who is constrained by the love of Christ.
- The combined operation of faith that works by love begins in the thoughts.
- Purity creates clarity. Clarity creates a voice in the Spirit. A voice in the Spirit creates a doorway of utterance. A doorway of utterance creates a breakthrough.

ENDNOTES

1. http://en.wikipedia.org/wiki/Artificial_respiration. Accessed 10/12/08.

2. James Strong, *The New Strong's Expanded Exhaustive Concordance of the Bible: Strong's Expanded Hebrew and Aramaic Dictionary.* (Nashville, TN: Thomas Nelson Publishers, 2001), 258-259.

3. Ibid., 108.

4. Ibid.

5. Please listen to CD Series, "The Timeless, Eternal Realm," by Warren Hunter, for more information on this subject.

Chapter Five

Christie in You

THE LANGUAGE OF THE SPIRIT

When the day of Pentecost came, they were all together in one place, Suddenly, a sound like the blowing of a violent wind came from heaven and filled the whole house where they were sitting. They saw what seemed to be tongues of fire that separated and came to rest on each of them. All of them were filled with the Holy Spirit and began to speak in other tongues as the Spirit enabled them. (Acts 2:1-4 NIV)

When the people mentioned in the above passage first experienced the infilling of the Holy Spirit on the Day of Pentecost, God was anointing them with power and authority. When the apostles and early Christians received the gift of the Holy Spirit, they received God in His fullness, not a piece or part of God; rather, everything He is and everything He has was imparted to them. Through the power of the Holy Spirit, they had gained access to God's mind, His way of thinking, speaking, and doing. In Second Corinthians 5:17 we read that "whoever is in Christ is a new creature." The word

Christ comes from the Greek word *Christos*[1], which coincides with the Hebrew word *Messiah*. This word literally means "anointed." Therefore, whoever is in the Anointed One and His anointing is a new creature. When a believer hears the word *Christ* or *Messiah*, they immediately think of Jesus, as they should. However, it is important to note that the kings mentioned in the Hebrew Scriptures, especially Saul, David, and Solomon, were also "messiahs," or anointed leaders, men chosen by God to be the head of His kingdom. To be anointed implies to be endued with the power to enforce the law of God and the authority to lead and shepherd a nation. This authority was given to David and his descendents.

When Jesus came to earth, we see the ultimate Christ, the One who would not only rule over Israel, but to whom all the nations of the earth would give their allegiance. Christ's authority included all peoples everywhere; He had been given the power to accomplish the law of God in every aspect and way, and the authority to be King of kings, Lord of lords, and High Potentate over every nation, tribe, and tongue. This is the authority that has been given to all believers by the infilling of the Holy Spirit. The same anointing that rested upon Jesus now resides within us. It is the anointing oil of the Holy Spirit that gives us the power to enforce the law of love on earth and the authority to rule and reign as His delegated authority on the earth.

It is clear then from this understanding of what it means to be anointed, that when a person receives the Holy Spirit, he or she is giving up the old man to be conformed to the image of the Anointed One, Christ Jesus. To know that you are anointed by God, chosen to rule and reign, is a key step in retraining your thinking and expectation. In Acts 2, Luke records for us how the Holy Spirit fell upon the believers in Jesus; it is important to note that after the infilling of the Holy Spirit, thousands of Jews began to enter into the Kingdom of Heaven by believing on the Lord Jesus Christ. Before this time, there had been a general rejection of Jesus by the spiritual authorities, and even many of His disciples fell away and left Him, until all that was left were the 12 and a few women who served Him. At the very end, Matthew chapter 26, verse 56, tells us that "all the disciples forsook Him and fled." In death, Jesus was completely alone. However, after He was raised from the dead, His disciples began to grow, until there were 120 gathered together in the Upper Room, praying in one accord. After they had been filled with the Holy Spirit, they immediately began to preach and teach Jesus the Christ, and signs and wonders followed the preaching of the Word. The first century believers had left behind their old nature, and received a new one— that of the Anointed One and His anointing. They had literally become new creatures!

TONGUES AND INTERPRETATION

Acts 2 makes it clear that these new creatures then spoke a new creature language. (Please read author's book, *God Working With God* for more information!) Many places in the Book of Acts, when a person was filled with the Holy Spirit, the Scripture says, "And they spoke in tongues and prophesied." Because the believers had taken on Christ, His anointing and His nature in exchange for their old nature (which Jesus had nailed to the Cross), they also received the ability to speak the language of the Spirit in exchange for mere natural words. Not only did they speak a new creature language, but they also understood this language and began to interpret it prophetically. In order for there to be tongues and interpretation of tongues, there must be unity in the Spirit. As the believers received the mind of Christ, their thoughts and their words came into unity with the thoughts and the Word of the Spirit.

I have seen a pattern in the area of tongues in individuals all over the world: when we pray in tongues and interpret, there is a move in the Spirit, which builds a divine connection with God's mind, because "tongues" is the language of the Holy Spirit (see 1 Corinthians 14:14, and Jude 20). Through interpretation, we are tapping into what God is thinking and saying. It is important to see why the Church must have both praying in tongues and the interpretation of tongues. In many churches, there is an emphasis on either the language of the Spirit or an emphasis on praying in a known language, such as English. Many fail to see the benefit and wisdom the Body of Christ can gain from having both. When we pray in tongues, we are speaking forth the mysteries of God:

> *For he who speaks in a tongue does not speak to men but to God, for no one understands him; however, in the spirit he speaks mysteries* (1 Corinthians 14:2).

We could say that in one sense we are sowing mysteries into God with the desire to reap understanding. When we interpret, we are reaping the revelation we desire. The Book of Jude tells us that when we pray in the Spirit, we are building ourselves up in our most holy faith (see Jude 20). In First Corinthians 14, we learn that when we interpret, we are building up the Body of Christ. Paul tells us clearly: I will pray with the Spirit and I will pray with my understanding. The key here is the word *understanding*:

> *I will receive with my understanding what I am declaring in the Spirit, speaking it forth into the atmosphere, so that my mind will receive it. I will believe it, receive it, and I will act upon it. My heart will be in harmony with my head, and my conscience will be connected to God.*

What will happen when my heart and my head come into harmony and receive with my understanding what I am speaking by the Spirit? I am going to receive the fullness of the interpretation of what the Spirit is praying out of me. The interpretation of tongues will bring correction to any false way of thinking or lies that a person has been meditating on; when a person receives this correction, the prophetic Word of God will help align that person's thoughts with the thoughts of God. Every time there is an interpretation of tongues and the prophetic voice of God comes forth, it will continually alter the thoughts of those who hear and receive what God speaks through the prophetic Word. I have seen the clear prophetic utterance of the Spirit alter the thought patterns of entire congregations! I was visiting a very poor area of South Africa in September of 2007, and God commanded me to speak in tongues and to interpret what I had prophesied. When I began to speak in English, the prophetic word told the people that God wanted to break the spirit of poverty off of their community. I prophesied that if they sowed beyond their means as the Macedonians had done in the first century (see 2 Cor. 8:1-7), that God would make the fruit of their righteousness abound and change their entire community, not just in the area of finances, but in bringing the lost into the Kingdom of God. The people did give all that they could, even though the offering remained less than $20 at the end of the service. Since that time, the church has grown both financially and spiritually, and many people have seen their unsaved relatives come to know Christ. Because the people willingly received the prophetic utterance given in tongues, and acted upon what they heard, their lives were changed forever.

THE CONSCIOUSNESS OF THE SPIRIT

I believe it is likely that during the time of the Tower of Babel everyone spoke in a language equivalent to what was initiated by the Spirit on the Day of Pentecost, what we now recognize as praying in tongues. I do not personally believe that they spoke Hebrew, as some evidence suggests that language developed later. This equivalency to tongues was quite possibly the only language of the time. It is possible that because of the degree of unity which existed at that time, as they spoke to each other, the other person understood clearly. Genesis chapter 11 says,

> *And the Lord said, "Indeed the **people are one** and they all have one language, and this is what they begin to do; now nothing that they propose to do will be withheld from them"* (Genesis 11:6, emphasis added).

In his commentary, Adam Clarke explains the "oneness" of the people as "unity of design and sentiment."[2] In other words, God was saying, "Anything is possible because they are in unity." Is that not amazing? The sovereign God of the universe is making the claim that if we are in perfect unity, nothing can stop us. I think the unity factor is just one indication that tongues comes from a higher consciousness. A higher consciousness, or the consciousness of the Spirit, is the place where our thoughts become God's thoughts. This is a place where we have given up carnal and immature thinking and replaced it with God's creative, pure, and holy thoughts. Without God's Spirit being active, it would have been impossible for sinful men to be in perfect unity with one another; true unity is the product of God's grace. Truly, for there to be perfect unity among the imperfect men who wanted to build the Tower of Babel, there must have been something of God's mind at work in them. We see this same manifestation of unity in the New Testament, after the first disciples experienced the infilling of the Holy Spirit.

> *Now the multitude of those who believed were of one heart and one soul; neither did anyone say that any of the things he possessed was his own, but they had all things in common* (Acts 4:32).

The new believers were able to live in unity with one another because they were beginning to operate in the consciousness of the

Spirit, instead of mind corrupted by sin. In the very next verse, we find the answer as to how it was possible for thousands of baby Christians to be in unity with one another—Acts 4:33 tells us that great grace was upon them all. According to *Strong's Concordance of the Bible,* grace is "the divine influence upon the heart and its reflection in the life."[3] As God's influence increased among the believers, unity and love increased. As the thoughts and actions of the new believers became saturated with God's way of thinking and doing, harmony increased among the brethren. It is clear that as we receive the Word of God in our hearts, God's divine influence will increase in our lives; as His grace is multiplied to us, unity will be the natural and inevitable consequence of His grace.

When Moses gave the Torah (the first five books of the Bible), he was writing something from a higher level, but it was in a form that could be understood by man occupying a lower level—the perfection of God's mind being communicated to fallen human minds. We read in Numbers chapter 12 that God spoke with Moses face-to-face. He was writing from a higher level of consciousness, a place of intimacy with God, where God's ways ruled supreme. Though this is actually the extent of relationship that God desired with all of His children, the people rejected closeness with God, and asked Moses to be a mediator between them and their Creator. Moses therefore demonstrated a higher level of communication that took place between him and God, and that would soon take place between God and all those who had been filled with the Holy Spirit. The separation that lies between a holy God and unholy people, between a God of love and a world filled with hatred, between a God of unity and nations filled with discord, has been permanently destroyed by the restorative work of Jesus Christ and the coming of the Holy Spirit.

The separation of languages that God caused to take place in Genesis 11 we see being restored in Acts chapter 2 and throughout the entire Greek Scriptures. Through the infilling of the Holy

Spirit, God now makes His home inside of human beings. When we see unity in the Body of Christ, we are actually seeing God's system working to unify God in Heaven with God in us. The Bible teaches us that God cannot be in unity with sin, compromise, or death. God can only be in unity with what He sees of Himself within His children (please read *God Working With God* for more information). There are actually many things in the Old Testament that represent a spiritual truth that would be brought to fruition through the life, ministry, cross, and resurrection of Jesus Christ. Through the blood of Jesus, we are restored to the higher consciousness that Adam and Eve functioned in before the Fall and that Jesus walked in His whole life. As Romans chapter 5 shows us by using a strong comparison between Jesus and Adam, we can see that Adam was symbolic of the second Adam who would restore all things, including man's mind, to its original perfection.

Nevertheless, the Old Testament has more than a symbolic value; it is the truth of God in every way. For instance, it is truth that Adam and Eve had to have more mental capacity in use than we do today. How else could they name every animal? In all likelihood, they communicated by using 100 percent of their minds. The communication could have been purely from a thought pattern, meaning they could have read thoughts. According to the Gospel of John, Jesus, who had an anointed mind, knew the thoughts of all men (John 2:24-25). Adam and Eve were crowned with honor and glory and also had an anointed mind—free from sin and impurity—that functioned at its full capacity. In this way, I believe they could have read each other's thoughts just as Jesus could read men's thoughts. This is the principle we see in First Corinthians 12, where the apostle Paul speaks about the gift of knowledge. This gift, initiated by the Holy Spirit, is when the Spirit of God reveals facts to a person about someone else in order to minister to that person or pray for that person. As we grow in our knowledge of God and His Word, it will be easy to hear what God has to say about other people and touch their lives with His love.

The Curiosity of God

Here is another perspective to look at: everything in the Garden was in absolute subjection to Adam and Eve. These two were not what we would call *normal people*. It says in Genesis 1 that they were made in the image of God! That means they had eyes like fire and feet like brass. It means they were like a flame of fire from the loins down and a flame of fire from the loins up. They had divinity living within them and manifesting through them and were completely dependent on God for everything—the way they looked, the manner in which they thought and communicated with each other and God, what they did with their environment, etc. Essentially, that means that whatever deception came into the Garden, their thoughts were clear to that deception, because they had God's thoughts and clarity on every issue. The thought conveyed was that if you eat the fruit of this tree, you will know the difference between good and evil.

Satan was trying to tantalize their minds.

How is this possible to a creature made in God's image?

If you were made in God's image, then you were created with a God-sized appetite for knowledge. You were made with a built-in, super-sized curiosity. You were created curious, creative, and interested in new things. You were created to know more, to grow, and expand. This was how Adam and Eve were created, but their consciences and inner man were without blemish or spot. Yet, even in perfection, they willingly gave in to the deception of satan with their minds wide open.

I was sitting with a prophet in his kitchen one day when a man called him on the phone. The prophet began to tell the gentleman on the phone where he was sitting, what he was doing, and what he had done. He read this guy's mail. I believe that if God can do this with a prophet today, He could have done that with Adam and Eve in the Garden. The Word says that God always creates a way of escape from sin. I believe they knew the clear communication of the deception of the enemy. After all, they walked and talked with God! They knew the Father's voice, His language, His way of communicating, as well as they knew their own—because it was their own! They knew God intimately in the same manner as God knows Himself. If another voice came along, certainly they would be able to recognize that it was not the voice of the Father that proceeded from their own mouths. Even with all this, they gave into the deception of the enemy.

I believe a lot of this had to do with their curiosity.

Really, the restriction that God placed on them was very small. In fact, God only restricted them from one tree in the center of the Garden. God gave them free access to everything else. So many trees to choose from, and yet they were drawn to the one which God had forbidden. This situation would be similar to a young child who is viewing an arrangement of clear balls lying on the floor, where one could see what was inside. If there were a single black one among them, the mind would immediately wonder what was inside the black ball. God says, "Do not look in the black one." But the mind would continually work to find out what was in that black ball. God had given them curiosity so that they would be continually hungering to know more about Him and be closer to Him, not in order to conjure up desires that God had forbidden. At some point they must have forgotten their curiosity for God and allowed their minds to wander to the one thing God had said was hands off.

We see this sort of distraction around us at all times. Satan sets up counterfeits of God's nature and character so that we will trade in our God-given desire for more of Him, and replace it with a drive to have the counterfeit. For example, we see that the enemy has permeated society with lust—any kind of sexual activity that takes place outside of marriage is lust. Any kind of sexual activity within marriage that is selfish and purely self-satisfying is lust. Any desire that takes you outside of the realm of trusting God is lust! The devil sets up the counterfeit of lust so that people—young people, especially—will continually seek to satisfy their insatiable desire for intimacy with

God with human solutions (i.e., pornography, fornication, masturbation, adultery, homosexuality, lesbianism, etc.).

People are hungry for the love and experience that only God can give; yet they seek the momentary pleasure of sin to silence the deep cry of their heart. They say things like, "I can't see God; I can't feel God. This I can feel!" It is the deception of the enemy. People struggle to meet their own needs through the counterfeit of self-promotion and greed because they are unwilling to receive what an invisible yet ever-present God offers them—namely, everything He has and is! Humans rely on the love of their parents, children, spouses, instead of leaning on the only love that will ever truly meet their need for love—God's! Satan wants people to turn their God-given curiosity and hunger for the Lord into a drive to obtain satisfaction in every other way possible. People fall trap to this very often.

Curiosity is a powerful tool used by God to birth creativity.

Still, curiosity is not a negative thing; it could not be if God created Adam and Eve with it, because God said what He created was very good. Curiosity is built-in in order to produce creativity. In order to be creative, people must first have curiosity to create something that has never existed. Curiosity helps to fuel our God-given desire to know more. The Lord placed it inside of us in order to spur us to search out answers to the secrets of the universe. It is curiosity that sets the small child to pulling apart an old radio or dissecting a dandelion to see what is on the inside of it. Even if a child has been warned many times not to touch the top of the stove, somewhere in their hearts they wonder, "And what will happen if I do touch it?"

The catch is that there has to be control over the curiosity in order to bring forth original ideas—ideas that are birthed in God.

Today, I believe that God by His Word is bringing us up to a new level of discernment. Yet even with the power available to us, God won't allow us to know the thoughts of all men unless our motives and attitudes are right and we are in a restored state. There will come a day when we will fully operate in the creative power of God. That aspect will grow in us. It has to be within the right boundaries, however. If God releases you to create planets or galaxies, just as He does, and yet your curiosity is not submitted to Christ, what God desires to bring forth will not be brought forth in His image. If He gave this great power and authority to a person who would not submit His will to God's, that person would be like God in power; in character; however, that person would be like satan. He is God and He wants someone just like Him, both in power and authority, and also in character. Many Christians today are following God in word, but in principle, they are following the enemy.

God is calling us out to a higher consciousness, but there are things that have to be dealt with before the gifts of the Spirit can have free expression in our life. In order for the curiosity of God to fully manifest its creative power through us, our hearts and minds must be pure before God and in unity with His thoughts and Word.

He wants your thoughts to be in harmony with His thoughts. When that takes place, the curiosity will not move in self-willed and unrighteous directions. This is why Romans chapter 1 says,

> ...concerning His Son Jesus, Christ our Lord, who was born of the seed of David according to the flesh, and declared to be the Son of God with power according to the Spirit of holiness, by the resurrection from the dead (Romans 1:3-4).

Jesus, the Son of the Most High, was not merely a Worker of wondrous miracles, a Diviner of wisdom and power—*No!* He was the Holy God of gods! Without holiness, there would have been no signs and wonders. They go hand in hand. When we walk in holiness, God will allow us to flow in His supernatural creative power; our aim will be to bring forth His perfect will, and not our own. We won't explore what we aren't supposed to explore. Learning to yield to the Father in the same way that Jesus did is a process. Even the Son of God, perfect and without blemish, was made perfect in the process of suffering (see Hebrews 2:10-18). There has to be a peace in your spirit about who God is in you—that we are truly nothing, and Christ is everything. Each believer must come to the place where they recognize what Jesus recognized: "I can do nothing on my own authority; as I hear, I judge; and my judgment is just, because I seek not my own will but the will of Him who sent me." Eve must not have had a peace that God was all He was supposed to be because she tried to exalt herself. The truth is her total reliance on God for everything, her utter union with Christ, her absolute abandonment to God's love, that high and exalted place of humility and adoration to God, was in actuality what it meant to "be like God." When the enemy came along and began speaking doubt to her concerning what God said to them, she allowed herself to be deceived. Paul said, "my children, do not be deceived. If you sow to the Spirit, you will reap of the Spirit" (see Galatians 6:6-8). If you sin, you are of the devil. In his first epistle, John teaches us that those who truly know God have given up their devilish ways. They actually **stop** sinning!

WHICH VOICE WILL CAPTIVATE YOUR THOUGHTS?

The enemy of our souls wants to continually remind us of the thought patterns that we experienced in the past. He wants us to identify with those thought patterns again so that we will return to them. Because we still live in the world, we are surrounded by reminders of what it was like to be *of* the world. The voice of Lot, which is the voice of the past that works its way into the Now to manipulate our future, must be cut off from our life before we can truly enter the Promised Land, our inheritance of freedom and blessing that God has prepared for those who love Him.

Lot is the voice of the past that works its way into the Now to manipulate your future.

Abraham, our father in the faith, had to separate himself from Lot before he could see and enter into the land which God had given him and his descendants. Lot, Abraham's nephew, had become a distraction from God's plan, will, and direction for Abraham's life. His presence was a source of irritation and frustration to Abraham. Lot was a voice in Abraham's life that continually reminded him of what he was and where he came from. Lot did not help Abraham to focus on the vision that God had given him. He was noise that hindered Abraham from doing the entire will of God. Because of the strife that was caused by Lot's presence, Abraham was finally forced to separate with him. Yet, it is clear that even in the separation, Lot took something away from Abraham. Lot chose to live in the best land, procuring the best fields for himself. Abraham's disobedience to God's call, which was to leave his whole family behind and go to the place God would show him, cost him in the end. In Genesis chapter 12, God told Abraham, "Get out of your country, from your family and from your father's house, to a land that I will show you." God specifically told him to leave his family behind, but he was not completely obedient; and because he did not follow God's instructions exactly he experienced problems in his future.

INTERPRETING THE HEAVENLY LANGUAGE

For this reason God has given us a heavenly language. He wants His voice to come out of our mouth so that we can meditate on what

He sounds like. Remember, faith comes by hearing, and hearing by the Word of God. If speaking in other tongues gives expression to the voice of God, then we are hearing the Word of God coming out of our own mouths. And, of course, the more we hear the Word, the stronger our faith will be. Our thoughts will be transformed from thoughts of doubt and fear to thoughts of faith and belief. I believe that God has a reason for speaking in other tongues. I believe that the more we pray in the Spirit, the more alertness and awareness concerning the things of the Spirit will take place in us. God intended for us to all speak one language in order for our minds and hearts to come into complete harmony and unity with His mind and heart and with the minds and hearts of our brothers and sisters in the Church. When we come to the place where each one of us is thinking God's thoughts, there will be no strife or division.

> *Even so you, since you are zealous for spiritual gifts, let it be for the edification of the church that you seek to excel.*
>
> *Therefore let one who speaks in a tongue pray that he may interpret. For if I pray in a tongue, my spirit prays, but my understanding is unfruitful. What is the conclusion then? I will pray with the spirit, and I will also pray with the understanding. I will sing with the spirit, and I will also sing with the under-standing* (1 Corinthians 14:12-15).

He is saying, when I first start praying in the spirit, my mind and my consciousness are not bearing fruit concerning what I am saying. That does not mean that I will remain unfruitful, however. He is saying I am making a start. The Spirit has to take over my conscious-ness in order for God's thoughts to completely replace the carnal consciousness that was part of life before salvation. Paul makes it very clear that you can only hold on to the mysteries of faith with a pure conscience. Jesus says very nearly the same thing in Matthew chapter 5: ***Blessed are the pure in heart, for they shall see God***. Do you see how these two verses are related? Hebrews 11:1 tells us, "Now faith is the substance of things hoped for, the evidence of things not seen." Purity has the ability to receive the things of God and hold onto mysteries beyond natural comprehension. The pure in heart are able to see the unseen, namely God. It is easy for God to relay His ideas, His very thoughts to a person who has a pure mind because God looks at that person and sees Himself. God loves to communicate His creative ideas to a being who not only thinks like Him but has the power inside of him to bring those ideas to pass. Only the person who is filled with the Holy Spirit, who has been anointed by God, who understands his identity in the image of Christ, is truly able to hold on to God's mysteries.

Tongues is yielded utterance springing from the Spirit of God within you, which voices what God wants to say.

Tongues is one of God's avenues for receiving and verbalizing God's thoughts. Interpretation is bringing the Word of God into a form that is understandable for my natural mind and the minds around me. Only a mind striving to be full of God's purity can receive God's voice and correctly interpret what God is saying. When I speak in tongues, the Holy Spirit within me is in touch with Heaven and He knows how to receive and how to verbalize God's thoughts.

Why do we interpret? When we interpret, the prophetic Word of God penetrates our ear to alter our thoughts and our minds so that we can believe and receive and act upon it. As we know from God's Word, faith comes by hearing, and hearing by the Word of God. When we speak the prophetic Word of God out loud, we will both be speaking it and hearing it at the same time. At this point our mind or our thoughts are now connected to our spirit and they come into agreement. The purpose for interpretation is to get our thoughts connected directly to the mind of God; they must become united as one in order to catch the heartbeat of God. How do we get our minds to harmonize? We get our minds to harmonize by praying in the Spirit.

> *For if I pray in a tongue, my spirit prays, but my mind is unfruitful. What is the outcome then? I shall pray with the spirit and I shall pray with the mind also; (I will receive the understanding of that which I am declaring in the Spirit and speaking it forth into the atmosphere, so that my mind will receive it. I will believe it, receive it, and act upon it.) I will sing with the spirit and I will also sing with the understanding* (1 Corinthians 14:14-15 NASB).

So, when I speak in tongues, I possess something that is not touched by the corruption of the carnal flesh. The interpretation of that word in an unknown language lines my thoughts and thinking up with the thoughts of God. The more you hear the voice of God speak through the avenue of tongues and interpretation, the more you will hear and speak God's thoughts. That means that I will not convey my own thoughts and my own ideas but only that which is of the Spirit. The Spirit will continue to keep me in touch with God; He will also help me to receive what God wants to say by interceding for me and making groanings unto the Father who is in Heaven. To do that, I have to continually pray in tongues no matter what I am doing. As I am going throughout the day, I should be communing with God by using my prayer language to enter into God's presence.

Previously we read Philippians 4:8, in which Paul admonishes us to meditate on the things of God, things that are pure and righteous and virtuous, instead of the filth of the world. What Paul is trying to do is get you to gear your conscience toward God, in order to create a clear pathway so that there is nothing of the flesh clouding your understanding. The process of setting your mind on heavenly things will help you to hold onto the mystery of faith with a pure conscience. Only a clear conscience can take hold of the mysteries of faith. Only when we have a clear conscience—one that is not constantly hindered by guilt and thoughts from the past, a conscience that is not over-shadowed by carnal thoughts—can we take hold and convey the thoughts of God.

When I speak in tongues, I am giving the Holy Spirit an audible voice to vent what the thoughts of God truly are. I am letting Him speak what God desires to speak and I am saying what God wants to say.

God's Spirit within us will always call those things that be not as though they are.

God has a voice—an audible voice that can be heard with the human ear. Adam and Eve, Noah, Abraham and Sarah, Moses, Joshua, Deborah, Samuel, Jesus, Peter, John, Paul, and others throughout Bible history and the present age, have heard God speak. Yet it is obvious from Scripture that God also wants to convey His messages to us through the mind of Christ and have us be the conduit for His Word. God created us to be His mouthpiece, His trumpet. He created us to be a living channel through which His thoughts could flow out to minister to the nations. Through the blood of Jesus, we have been restored to a place where we can flow with God again. We must, however, maintain purity in our thoughts. Thinking impure thoughts and meditating on impure things is like pouring grease down a kitchen sink. If it sits there long enough, that grease will harden into an almost immovable rock solid mass. Impurity will clog the conduit so that God's thoughts and Words cannot flow freely.

Thoughts of fear and doubt and indecision crystallize into weak, unmanly and irresolvable habits, which solidify into circumstances of failure, indigence and slavish dependence. Lazy thoughts crystallize into habits of uncleanness and dishonesty, which solidify into circumstances of foulness and beggary. Hateful and condemning thoughts crystallize into habits of accusation and violence, which solidify into circumstances of injury and persecution. Selfish thoughts of all kinds crystallize into habits of self-seeking, which solidify into circumstances more or less distressing.[4]

Let us look at this last statement: *Selfish thoughts of all kinds crystallize into habits of self-seeking.* We need to examine the activities we are involved with everyday. Why do we participate in those activities? What are we thinking about while we are doing those things? What do those activities help us to focus on? Is God the focus or do the activities we are involved with always point the focus back on ourselves? Do our activities foster thoughts of servanthood and the importance of giving, or do they conjure up thoughts of selfish ambition and greediness? If there is an activity in our lives that takes the focus off of serving God and others and puts the focus on "I, me, my," we need to know that the thoughts that are behind those activities need to be transformed. Our thoughts need to line up with what God thinks, and our actions need to line up with what God thinks.

On the other hand good thoughts of all kind crystallize into habits of grace and kindness, which solidify into sunny circumstances. Pure thoughts crystallize into habits of temperance and self-control, which solidify into circumstances of repose and peace. Thoughts of courage crystallize into manly habits, which solidify into circumstances of success, plenty, and freedom.

Energetic thoughts crystallize into habits of cleanness and industry, which solidify into circumstances of pleasantness. Gentle and forgiving thoughts crystallize into habits of gentleness, which solidify into protective and preservation circumstances. Loving and unselfish thoughts crystallize into habits of self-forgetfulness for others, which solidify into circumstances of sure and abiding prosperity and true riches.[5]

You need to focus your thoughts on the promises of God and not on your circumstances. God's thoughts are His promises. His promises are yea and amen. You need to know that *negative thoughts reverse miracles.* God does not know what it is like to think negatively. The devil uses the avenue of deception to plant seeds in our thought life that are the exact opposite of God's thoughts, Word, and will. Do not underestimate him—he enjoys planting thoughts that could very easily be misconstrued as God's thoughts; thoughts of false spirituality, pride, false humility, etc. are his specialty. His idea is to bring thoughts of fear into your mind that question God's goodness, His faithfulness, and His provision. Fear has the ability to hinder a believer's capacity to hear and receive God's Word. This is the devil's strategy: to get into your inner mind and stop God's thoughts, ideas, plans, and God's way of thinking from fully operating in your life.

OUR FATHER'S WAY OF THINKING

Jesus said, if you have seen Me then you have seen the Father. Jesus said, I do not speak My own words but the words of My Father, who is in Heaven. When I see Jesus, I see the way the Father would carry Himself. I see the way the Father would operate. I see Jesus say to the winds and the waves, "peace, be still." I see Jesus speak to the dead man and say, come alive. I see Jesus multiply the loaves and fishes. God's thoughts are higher than the rebellious and carnal thoughts of the unrenewed mind of the flesh. Like Jesus, however, we can possess the thoughts of the Father. We can say, I will only think what my Father thinks.

> *When you learn to become a lover and a forgiver, you will find the true riches of God.*

We need to get God's thoughts and not our own. Jesus said I was poor and you helped me; I was hungry and you fed me, naked and you clothed me (Matthew 25:36). Those are wonderful Scriptures. When we feed the poor, we need to do it our Father's way. When we minister to the needs of others, we should spend time in prayer to find out how our Daddy in Heaven wants to fix that problem. Remember, our Father does not solve problems in purely human ways. Our Father does not judge based on external standards. When the Israelites came to the Red Sea, God did not send a boat, or many boats, to get them across. God proved something to the Egyptians and the whole world that day. Our Father proved that He was a God of signs and wonders. He still wants to prove that same truth through our lives today. He is the same, yesterday, today, and forever.

I believe that the Holy Spirit has a grievance with the modern Church as to how we are representing and upholding the image of Jesus Christ. Though we are called to be His ambassadors, a city set on a hill that cannot be hid, we have watered down the revelation of God's love and power by offering the world man-made solutions instead of God's creative power. I believe that it is very difficult for humans to serve a God who offers them Heaven but cannot alter their circumstances in the now. We see this in America, Europe, and in the remotest jungles of the earth: there is a massive competition going on between the power of God and the "powers" of satan. Though many of us know and have seen the mighty power of the Sovereign God, thousands of people have not. These will ask themselves, "You say you serve a God of power; you say your God split the Red Sea. How do I know this is true if I never see any of this power in my own life?" They know about the power of darkness; they feel it around them at all times, controlling and manipulating their lives.

What do we offer them? Instead of teaching them about our Father who heals the sick and raises the dead, we have taught them about a God who saves their souls, leaves the rest of their beings to suffer through disease, depression, fear, anxiety, demonic attack, and finally, death. Unless we believe God is a powerful, supernatural God, we will never see His power manifest in our lives, nor in the lives we are trying to reach. If we are powerless, then we produce powerless people. It should be the desire of Christians to produce new believers who think, talk, and walk just like their Father God. It is inevitable that we will breed after our own kind. The question is what image are we reproducing? Is it the image of the Almighty God, or an image we have created ourselves?

A good example of this happened in our ministerial school, Supernatural Leadership Training Institute. We have had many people complete our courses, and all of them testify to the life-changing power of a training program that actually teaches people how to flow in signs and wonders. One powerful testimony comes from two young men, both in their 20s, who completed SLTI. They were in a severe car accident together, where their car crashed into a cliff while going 80 miles per hour. Because of the angle of the curve, the young man driving was killed on impact, while the other received only minor injuries. At the moment of impact, the young man went unconscious but woke up again very soon to find his friend dead. "Because of what I had been trained to do," he told me later, "I felt belief rise in my consciousness. I knew that God wanted me to raise my friend from the dead. Through SLTI, I learned that all things are possible to him who believes, and I had seen Brother Warren lay hands on many people who received their healing. So I just reached over, laid my hands on my friend's chest, and said, 'I command your breath to come back into your body! I command you to live in the Name of Jesus Christ!'" Immediately his friend started breathing again. When we raise up a generation of young people who know who they are in Christ, we will see them begin to empower others to do great and mighty signs, wonders, and miracles for the Kingdom of God.

Feeding the people with the grain brought from America will fill their stomachs; however, it will not necessarily demonstrate God's omnipotence. Multiplying loaves and fishes would demonstrate to them our Father's way of thinking and doing things. Though God often uses people to bless others, it should be understood that God does not need grain to make bread. God does not need human means to produce the supernatural. All God is looking for is a heart like His—one that thinks like Him, speaks like Him, and is completely yielded to Him. God does not merely offer humans Heaven after death, but Heaven on earth *now!* Starting off an evangelistic trip with a powerful sign, such as multiplying loaves and fish, would cause thousands of people to get saved in a very short amount of time, instead of taking years and years as it has in many countries. This is the difference between the human way of thinking about things and our Father's way of thinking about things.

I believe that Jesus knew what He was praying when He said in John 17, "Father, the glory that You gave me, I give to them, that they may be one just as we are one." Today I hear people say that we have only a fraction of the anointing that He had. As if you can take one drop of the anointing of God, and because it is only one drop, that somehow limits the omnipresence, omniscience, and omnipotence of God. Whether it is just one drop of God, or a bucket, God is the same. Who can measure God? In our minds we have tried to. We try to say God can go only so far. He cannot do more in and through me than that. I have heard people say, "Are you sure He can multiply loaves and fishes through me? I can't believe that. I might be able to lay hands on a few sick people and headaches will leave. But are you sure I can lay hands on people and raise the dead?"

Think Like God

God's thoughts are not our thoughts. His ways are not our ways. We have to be willing to give up our own limited thinking for God's bigness. God is not looking for people who think they have it all together. He is not looking for those who think they are powerful. The Scripture says that God makes His dwelling among the humble and contrite of heart. If we are willing to recognize that God is our source and we are nothing without Him, He will willingly use us to do the impossible. He knows then where the credit will go—to Him. Only by tapping into our Father's thoughts and our Father's way of doing things will we be a help to God in moving His Kingdom forward. We have to move it forward in God's way, not our own way.

LET THE ANOINTING FLOW

In order to further see why and how God wants to allow His thoughts and Words to flow through us, let us look at some of the simple men and women in the Bible that God used. By looking at their lives we will see what potential we have, if we will only allow God to rule and reign through us.

Paul the apostle is an excellent place to start. Remember, Paul (then called Saul) persecuted the church of God, condemning many to death. He took part in the death of Stephen, the first martyr of the Church. After Jesus knocked Paul off his horse on the road to Damascus, Paul was a transformed man. He healed the sick, gave sight to the blind, caused the lame to walk. Many other miraculous works were done by Paul. Demons were cast out with a handkerchief from Paul's body. That does not sound like limited power to me. Paul must have been meditating on God's abilities and not his own. Think about what must have been going through his mind. I am convinced by reading the writings of Paul that he knew from an early stage that God had given him an anointed mind. Christ, the hope of glory, was in Paul. Christ, *the* Anointed One's anointing, was dwelling on the inside of the man of God. We see this demonstrated in Acts 14:8-10:

And in Lystra a certain man without strength in his feet was sitting, a cripple from his mother's womb, who had never walked. This man heard Paul speaking. Paul, observing him intently and seeing that he had faith to be healed, said with a loud voice, "Stand up straight on your feet!" And he leaped and walked.

Paul was operating in the mind of Christ. He merely had to look at the man to know that he had faith to be healed. This is called discernment, which can only be accessed by those who are yielded to the Holy Spirit. It is the anointing within a person that gives that person access to the deep things of God. The anointing is all-powerful. In the anointing dwells the fullness of the Godhead bodily. When I am ministering in meetings, I want to be conscious of the very thing that held Paul's mind captive. I feel the Holy Spirit. I know what God in me is capable of accomplishing. Staying conscious of power, anointing, and the glory flowing out of us will keep our thoughts in line with what God wants to do through us.

Stay conscious that there is something tangible in you that the Father wants to impart through you.

The anointing in us is responsible for producing the glory. Yes, you are a son of God! Make this your meditation. When our thoughts are consumed with who God is and who we are in God, then we can operate in that manner because we are gearing our thoughts to that. The problem in the Body of Christ today is that we do not correctly perceive who God is, nor do we correctly discern the Body of Christ. Until we see God through the eyes of His Word and not through the eyes of traditions of men, we will not see ourselves through the eyes of God's Word. As we truly perceive who God is and what our incorruptible and undefiled inheritance is in Him, we will be able to fulfill

God's highest calling on our lives, and release the tangible substance of God's nature and character in our lives.

A catastrophic event takes place when we refuse to think about ourselves in the manner that God thinks about us. When we refuse to tap into the Father's thoughts toward us, it hinders us from seeing our potency in the Spirit realm, the authority that God has given us. Instead of just yielding our bodies as vessels and living sacrifices, allowing God's anointing oil to simply flow out of us, we will become proud in thinking that we can control God's movement or that God needs our assistance in order to flow freely through us.

Sometimes we do this by anointing a prayer cloth. We have to anoint the handkerchiefs before we can put them on someone. We get the "mail-order" prayer cloths that are anointed with special oil. We spend our money to get a piece of cloth that has been "specially anointed" with oil, when we forget that God's anointing oil can flow out of our very being. What a great money-making idea! It is man's idea, however, not God's idea. Nowhere in the Bible does it say that you need to anoint the prayer cloth in order to heal the sick. Even in James where it says, "If anyone is sick among you, let him call the elders of the church, and let them anoint him with oil, and the prayer of faith will save the sick, and the Lord will raise him up" (see James 5:14-15), we see that it is the prayer of faith that saves the sick, not the oil! We think we need to put oil on the prayer cloth to help the Holy Spirit out. The oil and the prayer cloth are only symbols of what we are carrying in our bellies already.

Oh, how easily we forget that we are the temple of the Holy Spirit! Our bodies are created to emanate the tangible presence of the Holy Spirit. So we have to help the Holy Spirit out to make it a little more tangible; we feel it must be understandable for the mentality that we are comfortable operating out of. We need to believe that the Anointed One and his anointing are living in us and through us. When we touch someone, God is touching them. We need to be less concerned with anointing prayer cloths with olive oil, and more concerned with allowing the real oil of the Holy Spirit to flow out of us. We need to really catch the heart of God and do what God has called us to do. We have to get our consciousness to understand that there is an indwelling anointing. We have a treasure in earthen vessels that the excellency of the power may be of God and not of man. He does exceedingly abundantly according to the power that is working in us.

> But you have an anointing from the Holy One, and you know all things....But the anointing which you have received from Him abides in you, and you do not need that anyone teach you; but as the same anointing teaches you concerning all things, and is true, and is not a lie, and just as it has taught you, you will abide in Him (1 John 2:20, 27).

There is a confidence that develops as a person allows the tangible anointing to flow through his life. At first it can be a little daunting, because you will be stepping into a realm you have never visited before; it is the realm of the supernatural thoughts of God. At a revival meeting we held a few years ago, I prayed for a lady who had a curled up little arm. I took her arm and I ripped it as hard as I could and pulled it straight up. I knew on the outside it looked out of order, but I was hungry for a miracle! I was just going to go for it all. When I did that, she screamed for about a minute. I pulled her arm down. The pastor was there and began to say, "This is it, Brother; you are going to be sued." I knew in my heart she was going to have a miracle, so I did not even stop to listen. I pulled her arm down and lifted it up again, and I knew that she had a miracle. She started crying and moving her fingers. Her entire arm had come out. Her fingers were straight. Her arm grew about an inch or two.

Then the ministers who had been watching realized what had happened. They went directly from doubt to belief. I saw something that day about thought. It is amazing how quick people respond. Their thoughts came out of their mouth as quickly as lightning flashes. When she screamed, they immediately expected trouble. They were thinking way down the road already. The ministers who were standing beside me said, "You broke her arm; this is it, Brother; you are going to be sued." Where was their faith? My thinking about the situation was geared toward God's power and love for this lady. Their thinking was not. Their thoughts were geared toward their own past failures and lack of results. Because they did not think of themselves in the fashion that the Father thought about them, they began to think that same way about me. But I refused to be moved by unbelief and pride. When we get the thoughts of God and we line our actions up with the Word of God, God's voice will come out of our mouths, making even other people's bodies line up with the Word of God. God wants to use our minds and our mouths as conduits for His thoughts and Words.

*Let God's supernatural thoughts of love rule
and alter the natural.*

If we can just get His thoughts, then it will be a lot easier for us to usher in the presence and glory of God. There are times when we have attempted to carry the Ark of the Covenant into the city on an ox-cart as they did in Second Samuel chapter 6. Yet, in this way they were disobedient to God; God had commanded that the ark be carried on the shoulders of the priests and not be put on any cart or thing made by men. This same disrespect for God's ways is demonstrated in our churches today. We want God to show up, but we do not take the time to do things God's way. We put pinball machines and video games in the church to get the teenagers off the street and into the church. We use the world's methods to get them saved. We are too lazy to go out, get them, cast the demons out of them, and get them saved. We have a God-given desire to see their lives changed, yet we forget that God knows best how to lure those who belong to him. We need to let them see real power. They need the real thing. If they cannot find the real thing, they will go someplace where they can experience real power. It is for this reason that there is such a widespread satanic movement among young people. The youth of this nation are hungry for power; because of style, hair color and length, and clothing preference, they have been rejected by the Church; the Church offers them rules to live by but no power to change. Instead, they turn to a power that offers them control and results—namely, the devil. If the anointing lives inside of us, however, we should be able to produce results for these kids. They are being deceived, and the Church is doing very little to stop it. We must lay down the traditions of men in order to become God's voice to this generation.

One time during a meeting I heard the Spirit of God tell me to walk off the stage into air and people will be healed. The height of the stage got to me. I began thinking not of the people having miracles, but of I, me, and my. "If I step out and fall down, I will be hurt." This was the voice of fear. The thoughts that were controlling my thinking at that time were thoughts of self-concern. I was more concerned with what would happen if I took the risk than I was about the people who needed the miracles. I did not let the thoughts of God rule. I rejected the supernatural and allowed the natural to be in control. All of us have faced situations like this one. For some, the request that God makes on them is small; for others it is large. Either way, believers are being tested to see if they really believe what God's Word says about the God they serve and about them.

DESTROY THE LAST DESTROYER

Love is more concerned about the people having the miracle than about the price of obedience and the risk of failing. If you focus on the miracle and on the supernatural, then you will do it. I learned a lesson from that. God gave me a dream that night of me walking out as I was supposed to and people were healed. I said, "Lord, why did I not see that?" As believers, we need to identify what is keeping us from seeing clearly what God says about us. What is the barrier in front of me that is hindering me from being all that God created me to be? I believe we should confront ourselves on this issue and ask, is the cost so great that I can afford not to do God's perfect will? We need to understand that never stepping out in faith is much more costly than doing things God's way. We need to know the devil's tactics. *We need to get our thoughts lined up with the Word of God and the things of God.* We need to do what God has told us to do. God will have you do things that you have never thought about.

The enemy of our souls is doing his best to distract us with fear and doubt so that God's thoughts will not manifest fully in our lives. He does not want you to catch what God is trying to say to you. I have seen all kinds of radical things happen in services, and God has asked me to do many radical things in order to see miracles take place. When I am ministering God's power, sometimes God tells me to punch a person or to pour water on a person. I have grabbed people in wheelchairs and yelled at them, "Just run!" Many other ministers of the Gospel have done similar things. One such minister was a man named Smith Wigglesworth. He was an evangelist in Great Britain at the turn of the last century. He had many tactics that people found strange and out of place. He punched people in the stomach and threw dead bodies against walls. Yet, God used his unusual ways, and even commanded him to do even stranger things! If you let God take over, you might see someone in a grocery store, and you might just grab them by the hand and rip them out of their little cart. You may not even know why you did it. You merely remained in obedience to the thoughts of God.

> *Let the words of my mouth and the meditation of my heart*
> *Be acceptable in Your sight,*
> *O Lord, my strength and my Redeemer* (Psalm 19:14).

We must recognize that God can only accept God. God can only receive God. If it is not of God, then God cannot work with it. The prayer of my heart as a minister of God is, let my every thought and word be in line with You, Lord. Let them be accepted by you, Lord. Let it be the way that You want it to be, Lord. We want our thoughts to be acceptable. We want to have an excellent spirit. We want our inner life and thoughts to be renewed and fully yielded to the Word of God. As our thoughts begin to line up with the thoughts of God, we will see the same creative power that flows through God begin to manifest through us.

In chapter 139 of the Book of Psalms, David is receiving a revelation about God and His character and nature. Remember that David is in the Old Covenant.

> *O Lord, You have searched me and known me.*
> *You know my sitting down and my rising up;*
> *You understand my thought afar off....*
> *For there is not a word on my tongue,*
> *But behold, O Lord, You know it all together*
> (Psalm 139:1-2, 4).

Before I even speak a word, He already knows my thoughts about it. Jesus knew the thoughts of all men. God knows what we are going to say before we even say it. One of the words for thought is *neoma*, which means a purpose or device of the mind. Jesus knew the *neoma*, the purposes and the devices of the mind and its rendered thoughts. Jesus understood the way in which the mind functions. As the Creator of man's mind, Jesus knew the potential of a man's thoughts. He was there when Adam called all the animals by name, speaking their destinies over them. He knew, as His Father did, that after the Fall, man's thoughts were continually evil. Christ is the one who gave Paul the ability to look into the heart of the lame man and see the faith to get healed. As a man thinks, so is he. Do you think that Jesus the healer lives in you? Do you think that you are above and not beneath? Do you think that you are the head and not the tail? Have you set your mind on things above and not on things beneath? As far as the world is concerned, you have died and your life is hidden with Christ in God. Our lives should reflect the truth that He who knew the hearts of all men and only thought as His Father thought now dwells in and possesses us.

> *Your eyes saw my substance, being yet unformed.*
> *And in Your book they all were written,*
> *The days fashioned for me,*
> *When as yet there were none of them* (Psalm 139:16).

God already wrote down your days before you even had any! That means that God thought about you before the foundations of the world. You are a word from the Word, chosen and known by God before time began. Your origin is in the Word; therefore, you are destined to think like God! (Please listen to, "Timeless, Eternal Realm").

> *How precious also are Your thoughts to me, O God!*
> *How great is the sum of them!*
> *If I should count them, they would be more in number*
> *   than the sand;*
> *When I awake, I am still with You* (Psalm 139:17-18).

If we do not know God's thoughts, they will not be precious to us. If we do not understand God thoughts, they will be of no value to us. But when we learn to receive the thoughts of God, we will begin to value them. What is David counting in verse 18? He is counting the thoughts of God toward you and me. That means that God has more thoughts for me than there is sand. Our desire should be to become intimately acquainted with the thoughts that God has toward us; in this way, we will sharpen our weapon against the enemy's lies.

Search me, O God, and know my heart!
try me, and know my thoughts!
And see if there be any wicked way in me,
and lead me in the way everlasting!
(Psalm 139:23-24 RSV)

God's desire for us to think His way is not a new thing; rather, He has always wanted His children to tap into His pattern of thinking and doing things. He did it with Abraham. When God showed him the stars, He wanted to see if Abraham had really seen a nation coming out of Isaac. He said, "Look at the stars, Abraham. Can you see what I see? I see millions of sons and daughters—more than can be numbered, coming out of your son Isaac. This is the direction My thoughts are going. Are yours going there too?"

Abraham's clear picture of the promises of God coming to
pass caused Him to penetrate past all natural barriers to
the place of fruition.

Then God tested Abraham. He said, "Go sacrifice Isaac." What was God saying? "Let Me test your thoughts, Abraham. Let Me see if you really have an inner image of what can take place by believing Me." This inner image was a God-birthed imagination. God was asking Abraham if he could see his children as numerous as the sand of the sea in his thoughts. Hebrews 11 says that Abraham received Isaac raised from the dead so as to speak in an inner image. Abraham's thoughts had become so permeated with the image of God's promise, that in his thoughts he had already seen Isaac raised from the dead. Abraham's thoughts had created such a clear picture of a nation coming out of Isaac, that in

Abraham's thought life, he had already seen past death! He had meditated on the stars so much and on God's power to bring His Word to pass, in his mind the power of death had already been broken off of his son. Abraham fully intended to stab Isaac, because his thoughts had already seen God's answer and power to overcome death. His thoughts penetrated past the realm of death.

Abraham was not only able to see the resurrection of Isaac; he had seen so far that he could see all the way to the day of Jesus Christ, and he could say to his son, "God will provide for Himself a lamb." The ability that Abraham received from God concerning Isaac is the same vision that God brought forth through the perfect sacrifice, Jesus Christ. The Scripture says that death could not hold Him. Jesus' knowledge of His destiny is what broke the bonds of death off of His life. He was destined to be King of kings and Lord of lords; Jesus saw past death to His resurrection.

VISUALIZATION BRINGS MANIFESTATION

What image comes to mind when I say the word *promise*? What things has God promised to you specifically that you are waiting on? Let me ask you this: What are you meditating on? Do you picture that promise coming to pass when you think about it, or do you doubt God? Can you see your miracle? Can you see yourself coming to harvest? Can you see yourself being all that God wants you to be? The vision has to come. Those visions are vital to what God wants to do. The thoughts have to come. The mind of God has to come. The Book of Joel says that God will pour out His Spirit upon all flesh. Your sons and your daughters will prophesy. Your old men will dream dreams. Your young men will see visions. Thoughts can come in picture forms that help you visualize your future. Can you see that new house in your mind's eye with the horse barn and the willow trees? Can you see yourself walking again after 15 years in a wheelchair? Can you see your child getting saved and free from alcohol and drugs?

There are times when I am ministering that the Spirit will begin to tell me in detail the problem within a person; yet even as I see the problem, it is as if the vision of Jesus takes over. I will see that person already lying on the ground or I will see someone in a wheelchair running around. That thought came in the form of vision; I could see the person healed in my mind's eye. Your young men will see visions. Did He say one vision or did He say visions? When God pours out His Holy Spirit, you will see visions. We must continually increase in our ability to visualize God's plan for our lives. Ask the Holy Spirit to open your eyes in the Spirit realm in order to see the God-destiny that God has prepared for you.

> *Having the right vision and maintaining a*
> *focused mind is the key to reaping the harvest*
> *you are expecting.*

Every week it seems like I am having a new vision. God is continually purging out the trash of my past and the influence of the world from my mind that I received through past mentalities and false thought processes. The more those ideas, philosophies, and traditions that are not of God are purged out of my consciousness, the more God will establish His vision. Developing God's vision for our lives will open the door for God to reveal more of Himself to me through dreams and visions. The dreams are really God's thoughts, and even when I am asleep, those thoughts will begin to dictate to my consciousness. When I sleep at night I dream about creative miracles. I see myself operating in God's creative power to touch the nations of the world. The only way this can take place is if, during my waking hours, I am setting my mind on things above, taking my thoughts captive, and casting down vain imaginations that do not come from God's Word. Once your waking hours are ruled by the Spirit of God, the devil will try to take advantage of you while you sleep. It is important to confess the Word over your mind before you go to sleep. This will guard your mind and heart from the attacks of the enemy while you are resting.

The greater the clarity of thought and clearness that comes to my mind, the greater and more perpetual visions will come to me.

Visions that are birthed out of God's thoughts and meditations will bring greater clarity to your thought life all the time. It is ultimately important that you are not meditating on other things that help to establish the thoughts of the devil. Secular media will establish the vision that satan is trying to set before you. If you are not filling your mind with the Word of God, then you will pick up visions that are contrary to God's Word. Many times the words that the devil sows are not purely demonic. Many times, the words are a mixture of God and the enemy. This is what makes him so dangerous. The enemy twists the truth, so that his lies will look attractive to the elect of God. Sometimes I will see someone who is generally anointed, who speaks anointed words and flows in God's power once in a while, begin to dip into the soulish and demonic thoughts that come from ungodly influences such as secular sitcoms and news broadcasts. They think by using these "resources," they will appeal to different kinds of people. The truth is, however, they are only appealing to the devil himself. God's thoughts will appeal to God and produce God in the hearers.

We need God's thoughts for today. We need a now thought. It is important that each Christian study the Word of God and receive personal revelation so that he or she can have a personal revival. I believe that the majority of believers receive all of their teaching on Sunday morning or from Christian shows on TV. This is not what God intended. He intended for each believer to seek Him and have intimacy with Him through His Word. The traditions we received from our parents and others in our lives may not actually be what the Word of God teaches on the subject. Each Christian must search the Scriptures, as the Bereans did when Paul spoke to them, and find out if what we are being taught is God's Word or traditions of men.

> *Beware lest anyone cheat you through philosophy and empty deceit, according to the tradition of men, according to the basic principles of the world, and not according to Christ* (Colossians 2:8).

Christians must be able to recognize when the Church is being infiltrated by ideas that do not come from the Holy Spirit. Often these ideas come from the world. We pick up on the world's way of doing things because we feel it is more attractive than God's way of doing things. Love and holiness are always God's way and must prevail in every situation. Christians should have no tolerance for sin in the Body of Christ. Sin in Christ's bride will destroy her ability to be God's delegated authority on the earth. Sin stains the Church's ability to show forth the perfect image of God.

> *For in Him dwells all the fullness of the Godhead bodily; and you are complete in Him, who is the head of all principality and power* (Colossians 2:9-10).

THE THOUGHTS OF CHRIST

The fullness of the Godhead bodily dwells in the anointing. One drop of God's anointing contains all of God. He is omnipotent, omniscient, and omnipresent. Whether you have only a trickle or a stream of the anointing, or a gusher of God's power flowing through you, you have to realize that what you have is truly unlimited and can accomplish all that God desires. You are complete in the Father, the

Son, and the Holy Spirit. *Somehow there has been rudimentary teaching full of nonsense and men's ideas and philosophies that has stopped us from getting the consciousness of the mind of Christ and an anointed mind.* When men teach ideas that are truly their own opinion and merely traditions, they make the Word of God of no effect (see Mark 7:13). Many denominations believe, for example that the gifts of the Spirit mentioned in First Corinthians chapter 12 are no longer in operation. When pastors teach this, their congregations believe that those gifts are not available to them. They cannot access that part of God's nature and character. When preachers teach that sickness is God's will, and He wants people to die of terrible debilitating diseases, we are training people not to expect God to move in their circumstances. When ministers get in the pulpit and preach to their congregations that it is holier to be poor than to be rich, that Jesus was poor, so we should be poor, they are teaching their sheep that it brings God pleasure when they cannot feed their kids or pay their bills. This kind of teaching has stopped us from getting anointed thoughts and anointed ideas so that we can speak anointed words by the unction of the Holy Spirit. We see that what is mentioned in Colossians 2:8 is stopping people from understanding the fullness of the Godhead bodily. Teaching like this is still going on in the Body today. People are caught up with the traditions of men, which amount to nothing! This way of thinking and teaching has stopped us from getting arms and legs to grow. They have stopped us from getting thoughts of God and from moving in the power of God to do what God has called us to do. Jesus had to continually deal with the traditions of the Pharisees. He could tell that their thoughts were not in line with what the Father says.

> *Then behold, they brought to Him a paralytic lying on a bed. When Jesus saw their faith, He said to the paralytic, "Son, be of good cheer; your sins are forgiven you.*
> *And at once some of the scribes said within themselves, "This Man blasphemes!"*

> *But Jesus, knowing their thoughts, said, "Why do you think evil in your hearts? For which is easier to say, 'Your sins are forgiven you,' or to say, 'Arise and walk'? But that you may know that the Son of Man has power on earth to forgive sins"—then He said to the paralytic, "Arise, take up your bed, and go to your house." And he arose and departed to his house* (Matthew 9:2-7).

The Pharisees did not want to acknowledge that He was the Messiah. They were still investigating Jesus' validity. He was showing them through demonstrations of power that He was the Messiah. They had thoughts of jealousy and envy because they did not see this same amount of power operating in their own lives. They were the religious people of the day. Jesus knew their thoughts. They were saying this man does not have the authority and the right to forgive sins. As the Son of God, however, He did have that right. If their thoughts were not in line with God's thoughts, then they could not recognize what God was doing. They were so focused on themselves that they continually challenged God's chosen Messiah, because, like satan, they were jealous of His position in God and longed to exalt themselves above God's Word. This is the pharisaical thinking.

In other historical writings dated to the time of Jesus, you can read about two men who went around doing miracles as well. They would identify the demon in the person through communication and when they identified the demon, they would drive the demon out in the name of God. They had a specific revelation of God's name from the Old Covenant teachings. They knew the name of God. They actually had among the teachers of the law a group of people set aside who were assigned to identify and search out the Messiah, when He would come and who He really was. They knew that specific miracles would be done only by the Messiah when He came. Even though other people could perform miracles, these certain miracles would not be seen in Israel until the Messiah was sent by God. This committee would have to go to where the miracle was done and see if this miracle was a Messianic miracle. If it did not fit into the category of miracles done only by the Messiah, then they knew it was not the Messiah. Only the Messiah could forgive sins and cleanse a leper. The Pharisees and Sadducees could not do that. They could not heal the person who was born blind. The Messianic miracles separated Jesus from all the Pharisees that were doing miracles at the time. That is what caused them to recognize Him as the Messiah.

What made Jesus different from others was His thought life. Jesus continually meditated on the Words of His Father. Jesus did not consider the honor of men something to be sought after. Jesus was full of humility about who He was. He said, "I can do nothing of Myself. I do only what I see the Father doing" (see John 5:19). Jesus' thought life was full of purity and perfection. Out of the purity and clarity of His thoughts came the manifestation of His true power.

Remember, Jesus said, the works that I do also shall you do, and greater works you will do because I go to the Father. If Jesus knew the thoughts of all men and He tells us that we have to do greater works, then He must be instructing us to come into greater thoughts as well as greater works. If we get His mindset, then He will bring us to the place where words of knowledge, wisdom, and discerning of spirits will come to fruition within us. Why would God want to unveil things to us if we do not have the wisdom on how to minister appropriately according to the thoughts of God? Do we have the mind of Christ? Do we have the same Holy Spirit that Jesus has? Do we have an anointed mind? Nothing can be hidden from an anointed mind. The mind of Christ contains an unction from the Holy One who knows all things.

"For there is nothing covered that will not be revealed, nor hidden that will not be known. Therefore whatever you have spoken in the dark will be heard in the light, and what you have spoken in the ear in inner rooms will

be proclaimed on the housetops" (Luke 12:2-3).

There is nothing hidden that will not be revealed. Whatever you are thinking will manifest itself in actions. When there is a thought that is not dealt with, it will solidify itself into actions. Remember, we are today what we sowed with our thoughts and words yesterday. If we sow to the flesh, we will reap to the flesh. If we sow wrong thoughts, it will manifest in the flesh today. We would be talking and thinking a lot differently if what we whispered in secret was shouted from the housetops.

Whatever is coming out of your heart, whether it is to someone else or in the most secret place of all, will always find its way to the surface. It will affect your circumstances. When you open your mouth a lot, you always make your thoughts vulnerable. They are always open. That is why it is very important that you guard your heart, because out of it come the issues of life. Make sure you keep things in line with God's thoughts about you. Meditate on what God says about you, and do not commit yourself to the opinions of men.

> *But Jesus did not commit Himself to them, because He knew all men, and had no need that anyone should testify of man, for He knew what was in man* (John 2:24-25).

Jesus was full of the Holy Spirit and He could read men's hearts. He could read the thoughts of all men. God wants you by the Spirit of God to know the thoughts and intentions of the hearts of other people and what is really in them.

> *But the Lord said to Samuel, "Do not look at his appearance or at his physical stature, because I have refused him. For the Lord does not see as man sees; for man looks at the outward appearance, but the Lord looks at the heart"* (1 Samuel 16:7).

Remember, God looks at our hearts. He is looking into the inner man of who we are and what He has created us to be to find out if we are yielding to His thoughts or not. He is not moved by outward appearances or carnal strength. God is interested in what we do with His thoughts and Words. Are we abandoning ourselves to the Father's thoughts? Are we praying in the Spirit, building ourselves up in our most holy faith? Are we allowing the interpretation of tongues to align our thoughts with what God is thinking and saying? If we are, then we will find that God is pleased with us. We are really learning what it means to have the mind of Christ—an anointed mind that is full of God's love and God's Word. An anointed mind is focused on what God has to say and not on the material that the world and the devil are continually trying to throw our way. Our destiny is to have our minds conformed to the meek and gentle mind of the Lamb of God who did not consider it robbery to be equal with God, but made Himself of no reputation and took on Himself the form of a servant. This is a mind that allows God's anointing to flow freely through it without the hindrances of carnality and impurity. For God is seeking such minds to fill with His life-giving thoughts.

Think Like God:
GOD-THOUGHTS FOR MEDITATION

- I will receive with my understanding what I am declaring in the Spirit, speaking it forth into the atmosphere, so that my mind will receive it. I will believe it, receive it, and I will act upon it. My heart will be in harmony with my head, and my conscience will be connected to God.
- Curiosity is a powerful tool used by God to birth creativity.
- Lot is the voice of the past that works its way into the now to manipulate your future.
- Tongues is the spirit of God within you voicing what God wants to say.
- The Spirit of God within us will always call those things that be not as though they are.
- When you learn to become a lover and a forgiver, you will find the true riches of God.
- Stay conscious that there is something tangible in you that the Father wants to impart through you.
- Let God's supernatural thoughts of love rule and alter the natural.
- Abraham's clear picture of the promises of God coming to pass caused Him to penetrate past all natural barriers to the place of fruition.

- Having the right vision and maintaining a focused mind is the key to reaping the harvest you are expecting.
- The greater the clarity of thought and clearness that comes to my mind, the greater and more perpetual visions will come to me.

ENDNOTES

1. James Strong, *The New Strong's Expanded Exhaustive Concordance of the Bible: Strong's Expanded Greek Dictionary of the New Testament*. (Nashville, TN: Thomas Nelson Publishers, 2001), 273.

2. Adam Clarke, *Adam Clarke's Commentary*, Genesis 11:6. Power BibleCD. Bronson MI: Online Publishing, Inc. 1999.

3. Strong, 270.

4. James Allen. *As a Man Thinketh*, (St. Augustine, FL: AsaManThinketh.net. 2001), 13.

5. Ibid., 14.

Chapter Six

Calmness Is Power

CALMNESS

Every storm in history from the infamous hurricanes that have hit the Southern and Eastern States to flash floods around the world that have killed countless people—all have one thing in common: they all began with one single and seemingly insignificant drop of rain. If you could ask that individual drop of rain if it were responsible for any devastation, it would probably reply, "Who me? I'm just a tiny drop of rain." When a storm is at its full fury, few people even recall that first, single drop. But every storm had to have a beginning.

Sometimes our thoughts can become a storm. Just like any raging storm that begins with that small drop of water, our thoughts can seem insignificant at the beginning, only to produce raging storms that take on a life of their own. Once in a while a thought will come that we forget to take captive. That thought produces a pattern of thinking that produces the seeds of words. Those words can cause a storm—a hurricane that started with just one drop of water, just one unbridled thought. That's why self-control is such an essential part of our walk with the Lord. When we control our thoughts through the power of the Holy Spirit, our words will be bridled, causing great calmness and power. Death and life are in the power of the tongue (see Prov. 18:21). When things are out of control, you can begin to calm the most powerful storms by casting down vain thoughts and calming the storm that is in your mouth.

Self-control is strength. Right thoughts are mastery. Calmness is power.

Calmness is power. The Bible always speaks about calm in relationship to a storm—storms that are stirred up by people's thoughts, words, and actions. The Bible teaches that the Messiah, the Anointed One, calms the storms.

> *He calms the storm,*
> *so that its waves are still* (Psalm 107:29).

The anointing that was on Jesus, the Messiah, to calm the wind and waves, to say to the storm, "Peace, be still," is on our lives today as Spirit-filled believers. We have been anointed to calm storms and settle waves—not just physical hurricanes and tornadoes (though we can calm those too!), but also the storm of thoughts from the past that come against us, thoughts of confusion and unbelief that cause words of doubt. Self-control concerning one's thought life will produce self-control in other areas of life. Self-control in the thought life will produce a drive to have focus and calm in every part of our day. Self-control means that we set our mind on things above and not on things beneath; we must keep our minds focused on what God has to say about each situation and cast down every false thought that tries to work its way into our minds. In order to do this, we must yield control of our minds to the Holy Spirit. Self-control will manifest in our lives as we yield total control of our thoughts, words, and actions to the power of the Holy Spirit. It is not possible to have self-control without giving up our control to our Creator.

Once again, let us look at the physical body as a demonstration of our make-up in the spirit realm. The brain is the center of all activity for the whole body. Without the brain, a person cannot see, smell, hear, taste, touch, walk, talk, hug a friend, drive a car, eat a sandwich, or take a shower. Without the nervous system, all human activity is impossible. The brain is responsible for all physical actions, both those that are voluntary, and those that are involuntary. When your stomach digests food, it is your brain that is telling it to do so. When you bend your knee, it is your brain's instruction that caused it to happen. The point is, your nervous system is in control of what you do.

When you see patience taking the time to apply itself to self-control, you have seen the power of calmness.

In like manner, your thoughts are in control of what you *are*. You will never say anything that you did not first think; you will never become anything that you did not first meditate on. Even those actions that people assume are involuntary were thoughts before they were anything else. The tongue, as James tells us in chapter 3, verse 6, is sharper than a two-edged sword, and can set the course of nature on fire; yet it is powerless without the mind. We may as well look at our situations honestly—our thoughts are continually coming out of our mouths, dictating who we are and what we will become. Whatever thoughts are consuming our daily lives are going to end up in our mouths.

We have to allow God's thoughts and meditations of His heart to consume us, so that His purposes and ideas will be coming out of our mouths. God's ideas are creative and powerful. His thoughts are supernatural. His mind always operates in the "Conqueror" setting; He always maintains an "I can do it" mentality. His thoughts are consumed with love. The question is, what consumes your thoughts?

Think Like God

To what issues do you dedicate most of your brainpower? What do you meditate on during the day? It is important that you answer these questions so that you will be able to identify areas of your thought life that need to change. Take a moment to consider, and write down what the Spirit of God reveals to you.

A HARVEST OF CALMNESS

All thoughts are potential seeds, because your thoughts are where seeds are birthed. When your mouth speaks those thoughts, the seeds are planted and ready to grow. Your thoughts are the building blocks for your life, because what you think about will become your actions, which will produce certain results in your life, either good or bad. The Bible teaches us that we must guard our hearts with all diligence, because out of it flow the issues of life. Each believer must recognize that whatever is enthroned in a person's heart will be king in their life. If Jesus is the center of their heart, then He will be king. However, if fear is at the center of your heart, then fear will rule in your every decision. If some person and his or her opinion is enthroned in your heart, then what would please that person will be your deciding factor. It is obvious that the ideals you enthrone in your heart are what your actions will be calculated around. If all of your thoughts are centered around a particular ideal, each thought will be like a tiny seed planted in the fertile soil of your mind. When thousands of seeds are planted, they will produce vast fields ready for harvest. The same principle will take effect when we hide the Word of God in our hearts, just as David said in Psalm 119:11: "Your word have I hidden in my heart, that I might not sin against You."

The measure of thought that we apply to the Word that we receive will be the measure of virtue and knowledge that will come back to us.

If we allow the Word of God to be enthroned in our hearts instead of allowing in the foolishness of man's philosophies, we will see its virtue and knowledge multiply in our hearts like a mighty harvest waiting to be gathered in. If we value and meditate upon the Word of God, we will see its power come to fruition through us because we have taken its power seriously. We have considered the Word continually in our minds and made it our focus and desire.

> *A man will be satisfied with good by the fruit of his mouth,*
> *And the recompense of a man's hands will be rendered to*
> *him* (Proverbs 12:14).

How can a man be satisfied with the words of his mouth? True satisfaction comes for a believer only when God is pleased with that person. He or she may try to find satisfaction in the good opinions of peers or in the accolades of superiors, yet they will remain hungry for the pleasure of the Father. There is nothing that compares to hearing the voice of the Holy Spirit say, "I am pleased with you." God is pleased when we are watchful of the thoughts we meditate on and choose our words wisely. God is pleased when His children discipline their tongues to speak only what they hear Him speaking. True satisfaction will come when the believer thinks only upon the things God has said, and speaks only the words God has spoken. The result of the God-habit of speaking the Word is a God-harvest of God's nature and character in our lives. The seeds of God's Word that started in the meditations of His heart will be birthed into the earth through your mouth because you have chosen to meditate on Him instead of other things. God's harvest, the harvest that He preordained before the foundation of the world, will come to fruition because of your obedience.

> *But the tongue of the wise promotes health* (Proverbs 12:18).

He who guards his mouth preserves his life,
But he who opens widehis lips shall have destruction
(Proverbs 13:3).

A wholesome tongue is a tree of life,
But perverseness in it breaks the spirit (Proverbs 15:4).

A gentle tongue, with its healing power, is a tree of life.
But willful contrariness in it breaks down the spirit
(Proverbs 15:4 AMP).

The tongue of the wise uses knowledge rightly,
But the mouth of fools pours forth foolishness (Proverbs
15:2).

When we read verses like these from Proverbs, we have to be careful not to disconnect words and the fruitful use of knowledge from our thought life. Let's face it—a wise man does not manage to guard his mouth and use knowledge rightly without purifying his thoughts. In order for him to guard his mouth, unwise thoughts threatening to produce destructive words must be purged out. Only when a wise man purifies his thoughts will there be calmness and control to his mind, his tongue, and his life. Then he can take dominion over all the storms that arise because he does not have fluctuation in his thoughts or mind that causes him to waver and be uncertain.

And you, who once were alienated and enemies in your
mind by wicked works, yet now He has reconciled...
(Colossians 1:21).

Again, we cannot help but notice how God's Word links being an enemy in your mind with the wicked works it inevitably produces.

Wrong thinking makes a person God's enemy because wrong thinking produces wrong actions. After God reconciled us through the blood of Jesus, there should have been a massive adjustment in our thought life. At one time the thought pattern did not have God in mind at all. Our thoughts were set on pleasing ourselves and others. But now it has changed. Notice how Paul describes the same group of people in the epistle to the Colossians:

> And have put on the new man who is renewed in knowledge according to the image of Him who created him... (Colossians 3:10).

A wise man's calmness of mind reveals the fruit of a mental focus toward God's thoughts. It reveals a patient pursuit of self-control.

Far from being enemies, their minds have been renewed and transformed. God did the reconciling, but they were responsible to put on the new man and renew their minds by the washing of the water of the Word. Did the thoughts that previously made them enemies of God simply vanish? No, they did not. Though the power of those past patterns of thinking and doing things had been broken by the blood of Jesus Christ, they had a responsibility before God to renew their minds with the Word of God so that those patterns would not return to visit them. The devil's tactics are to continually try to bring up the sin/memories of the past so that the moment you really think you are free from them, he slings another arrow at you. The Colossians were under this same kind of attack, so Paul taught them the key to overcoming: complete and utter reliance on the Word of God. Filling their minds with godly wisdom would help them to overcome the attacks of the enemy in the same way that it helped Jesus overcome temptation. As they renewed their minds, they had to purge the old way of thinking and replace them with God's way of thinking.

And the peace of God, which surpasses all understanding, will guard your hearts and minds through Christ Jesus (Philippians 4:7).

Just as a warm day with calm and gentle weather promotes feelings of peace, the peace of God goes hand-in-hand with calmness. Remember that calmness is power. The Greek word for *peace* is *eirene* (i-ray'-nay) it means: "peace, prosperity, one, peace, quietness, rest. ."[1] Because this epistle was written by a Hebrew, it is also important that we study what the Hebrew words are so that we have the correct background and culture for this word. As Paul was a Hebrew of Hebrews, of the tribe of Benjamin (see Phil. 3:5), it would have been important to him that his readers understand all that God was offering them through His peace: the Hebrew word for *peace* is *shalom*, which means: safe, well, happy, friendly; and also speaks to welfare, health, prosperity, peace, and even favor.[2] God's shalom expands to cover every area of your life. From being in good health to buying a new home to being safe from enemies, the Lord's shalom, promised you through the blood of Jesus, should accompany you and every believer.

A good way to illustrate one key aspect of shalom is to picture a man going out to buy a new car. He chooses the color he wants and all the options he desires, and the total comes to $20,000. He double-checks his bank account and notices he has well over $20,000. He has enough for the car, with plenty left over to cover other expenses—super abundance, more than enough, and overflowing, are what God offers through His peace. The man can pay cash for the car, no leasing or borrowing, no credit applications or credit checks. This is a picture of great blessing and no stress. This is God's peace. Shalom means that nothing is lacking. This man has complete financial soundness. He has all the resources he needs to accomplish the desire of his heart.

God's peace offers complete wholeness where nothing is lacking. When we walk in the peace of God, staying calm in the face of storms is not difficult because we see the mighty hand of God making provision already, so that there will be nothing lacking.

STAYING FOCUSED

Once our mind has accepted God's shalom, it is then prepared to fully focus on God's thoughts. Our focus is the key: especially when it comes to allowing the Holy Spirit's anointing to operate in our lives. Like a satellite dish that has to lock into the right position to have good reception, the anointing also has to be brought into a position of maximum reception by our focus. That anointing, with the right focus, will bring results. If the anointing is focused on the truth of God's Word, that anointing will take on substance. On the other hand, a satellite dish that has not yet secured a good signal is still searching. It's also safe to say that until we get our thoughts locked in with the purposes and plans of God, there will be no fruitful or intelligent accomplishment. God's miracle working power is always available, but whether or not we experience it depends on our focus.

Until you get your thoughts connected with the purposes and plans of God, there will be no fruitful or intelligent accomplishment.

Focus, by its very definition is something continuous. Focus has staying power. The same satellite dish that catches a signal has to maintain it to relay a good picture. When snow, wind, or rain come along, they can cause a dish to lose good reception—despite its good positioning. In much the same way, negative thoughts try to destroy our focus on God's Word. They can even reverse miracles. Remember, as a man thinks, so is he.

Think Like God

Focus is a mentality of stick-to-it-iveness that hooks itself up with where God's thoughts are headed. It can see the pattern of God's thoughts moving toward a specific goal, just as a satellite tracks a signal and broadcasts it as it is actually happening. Focus is driven by desire to finish God's way. It is propelled by vision, an ability to see God's thoughts coming to fruition, even before it manifests in the natural. Focus knows how to break the barriers of doubt and unbelief that come its way through various avenues, because it gives those barriers no recognition. Nothing can stop a focus that is fueled by dreams and vision that have been given by God. It sets its eyes on what God has revealed, and never looks to the right or to the left.

> *And He said to them, "Be careful what you are hearing. The measure [of thought and study] you give [to the truth you hear] will be the measure [of virtue and knowledge] that comes back to you—and more [besides] will be given to you who hear* (Mark 4:24 AMP).

In other words, whatever measure of time, energy, and resources I am willing to put into a certain thing, that same measure is going to be meted back to me by God. As we apply this principle and meditate on God's miracle power, God will occasionally give us extraordinary instructions. I vividly remember a time when God's power was moving in a remarkable way. For a season, I had been giving my focus to hearing God's truth on healing. With the same measure I gave time, energy, and resources to God's healing power, I received revelation of God's healing power in my own life. While praying for the sick, I came across a man with a stomach problem. God clearly told me to punch this man in the stomach. At this point, a mind out of focus would raise all kinds of negative thoughts. Did I hear God correctly? What if this man dies afterward?

Thank God I kept my focus and simply allowed God's anointing to go in the direction the Spirit of God was leading! As I obeyed, I was not wondering about the outcome. I focused my mind on the fact that I was walking in obedience to the mind of Christ. I did not allow thoughts of doubt and confusion to enter in, questioning my ability to hear God's voice and do what He told me. After a brief moment when the man was in shock at this method, he was totally healed.

A lack of focus can produce numerous negative and destructive thoughts in a few minutes, because focus determines mastery!

Jesus focused on the joy that was set before him and endured the Cross. Jesus set the joy of God before His mind continually. What was the joy that Jesus meditated on? It was the knowledge that He was walking in perfect obedience to the Father. Hebrews chapter 12 even says that Jesus despised the shame of the Cross. The word for *despised* in the Greek actually means, "to think little to nothing of; to give no attention to; to look down upon."[3] Jesus set His face like flint so vehemently that He did not give one second of thought to the shame of the Cross. He cared nothing for it, because He set His eyes on joy. Jesus focused on God's purposes and not His own.

What are the things that God has spoken directly to your heart? What has God told you that He wants to accomplish through you? Meditate on those things, not on the circumstances that surround you. Let the promises of God fill your mind; set your face like flint toward what God says about you. Set your mind toward the joy of your salvation and calling. God knows our thoughts. We need to focus our thoughts on the promises of God instead of the circumstances.

It is important to understand the position we have been given in the Kingdom of God. A God-like focus comes from seeing every circumstance from God's perspective. We need to understand that we are seated in heavenly places. He has called us to rule and reign with

Him in Heaven and on earth. Always keep in mind that this is a position of sovereignty: we have been granted sonship, authority, and dominion. We have been clothed with the divinity of Christ. We are above and not beneath. As far as the world is concerned, we have died and our life is hidden in Christ with God. Set your mind on things above and not on things beneath. Focus on God's perspective: He sees things from the standpoint of continual and utter victory! He is the Mighty Conqueror over all the earth. We need to start thinking in supernatural terms and move away from the things of the natural.

Focus Fights Fear

Our mind is always working and learning and thinking. It has the ability to change directions very quickly. It has the ability to forget things that happened five minutes ago, and yet remember that one thing you would love to forget that happened 20 years ago. It is a powerful weapon God has given us against our enemy—and our enemy is going to spend every resource he has to steal our weapon from us and use it for his own benefit. When we fail to keep our focus on God, the mind does not simply go blank. The devil is constantly trying to establish his thoughts within us all of the time. Most of his thoughts involve some type of fear. Fear is the devil's number one tool for distracting us from focusing on God and thinking God's thoughts.

When Jesus and His disciples were in the middle of a storm, Jesus slept in the bottom of the boat. Jesus was not moved by the storm at all. When Jesus rose up, the first thing He did was rebuke their unbelief. Only then did He speak calmness to the storm. His calmness was power and strength for the disciples, even when He was not awake, and that power and strength remains for us today. Jesus never got worried or agitated. He never held unforgiveness in His heart, or yielded to violence or unrighteous anger. The disciples should have realized that the boat was not going to sink as long as the Promise was on board.

If the Promise is asleep on the boat, we have power riding with us. Many times it seems as though Jesus is asleep on our boat. It seems as though He is not answering, not making anything miraculous happen for us. I have found that at the times Jesus seems to be asleep, He is merely watching and waiting to see if we will step into our destiny as His image-bearers and do what He would do. Jesus wants to see how we will respond when a storm hits. Will we recognize that He has given us authority over the wind and the waves and that we can walk in the peace and the calm that He walked in no matter what is going on around us? Or will we revert to old patterns of thinking and doing? The choice is up to us. Everything we need He has already given to us through the anointing of His Holy Spirit.

Fear is false evidence appearing real.

Had Jesus allowed His focus to be sidetracked by fear and agitation, do you really think He would have been able to raise the dead? His disciples were very disturbed and agitated when they heard that Lazarus had died—Jesus, however, was not (see John 11:1-44). Jesus calmly stood up, raised His hands, and said, "Father, I thank you that you hear Me." Why did He thank God for hearing Him? He said this for the sake of the people listening, not for His own sake. Earlier in the same passage in the Book of John we see that Jesus was moved to tears. John chapter 11:35 says that Jesus even wept. Contrary to the opinion of some, Jesus did not cry for the death of Lazarus, His friend. He cried because of the unbelief of the people. They were anxious and agitated. He told Martha, "You are anxious for no reason." He was telling her to stay calm. Many of those around Him could not hear the thoughts of God because of their agitation. When we remain calm and at peace, it is much easier to hear God's voice with clarity. Calmness tends to produce the stability that comes with often hearing God's voice.

The devil is constantly trying to cloud our understanding by establishing thoughts of fear. These seeds of the devil's very nature will keep us from hearing the thoughts of God. In response, we need to find out what God has to say on the subject. What kinds of things fill the mind of God? God's mind is consumed with love. The Bible says, for God so loved the world that He gave us Jesus, the Lamb slain before the foundations of the world. God chose us in Him before the foundations of the world that we should be holy and without blame before Him in love. God is love, and all of God's purposes are wrapped up in love.

God's Word is a revelation of God's own thoughts.

Each person must recognize that he or she is part of God's love plan. If we see how we fit into the big picture of God's purpose, it will give us vision to break barriers. Vision creates focus, and focus determines mastery. If a man is focused, he has the ability to cast down thoughts of fear that say he is no good and will never accomplish the will of God for his life. He recognizes the strategies and tactics of the enemy trying to deceive him. The reason that the devil is so intent on convincing us that we are born to fail without any hope of success is because our victory is so inevitable and it scares him silly! He would not spend nearly as much time telling us that we are worthless if he did not already know that we are priceless! At times, the enemy will send people into our lives, even people that we love and respect, specifically to tell us that we cannot do it. Do not listen, friend. Do as Jesus did: set your eyes on the joy of victory that is ahead of you and do not give the lies of the enemy any of your time. Focus on God, and the love of God will drive you out of fear.

Do you ever wonder what God really thinks about you? Remember what the Word of God says about you. Search the Scriptures to find out who you are in Christ. Find out for yourself. God's

Word was birthed out of God's mind. It is a testimony of who God is and what He can do. It is His covenant of peace (shalom) between God and His children.

Thoughts are where seeds are birthed. Words are where seeds are planted. First you think about something, and then you do it. The Bible tells us to speak to ourselves in psalms, hymns, and spiritual songs, making melody in our heart to the Lord. That means, think diligently about what God's Word says about God and about you, sing the Word of God, and allow the Spirit of God to rise out of you to create new songs birthed from God's Spirit and God's Word. The reason for this instruction is to keep us ever mindful of the things that God is trying to say.

The thoughts of God are established in the mind of Christ.

Focus on the thoughts of God. There will always be three sets of thoughts that will try to take dominion over our minds: the thoughts of the flesh, the thoughts of the enemy, and the thoughts of God. We have to learn to discern who is speaking. When we discern God's thoughts, we will be able to speak an anointed word and see immediate anointed results. One anointed word packed full of the love of God can bust the bondages off a person that have been lingering and harassing him all his life. I have seen literally thousands of people over the past 20 years of ministry healed, set free, filled with the Holy Spirit, and set on fire for Jesus just by speaking an anointed word. God will tell you to do something that you would not normally think to do; the love of God is interested in doing whatever it takes to bring people closer to Him. Sometimes that takes drastic measures.

One such example of this happened in a revival meeting in Pennsylvania. I had an interesting encounter with a young man in one of my meetings. This young man was actually the son of a minister, and was attending the meetings only at the command of his parents. During the message God told me to take my glass of water, walk over to the boy, and throw the water in his face. The Holy Spirit said, "Say to him, 'This is what your Father says: "It's time to wake up!"'" Truthfully, I was shocked by what God wanted me to do; but instead of worrying about what would happen afterward, I simply obeyed: in the middle of my sermon, I left the pulpit and stood in front of the young man. I threw the water in his face, much to his surprise and to the surprise of his mother and the entire congregation. In a loud voice I said, "This is what your Father says: 'It's time to wake up!'" Then, as if nothing had happened, I continued with my message. A few weeks later I was back at my office and received a very interesting phone call. It was from the young man's mother. She told me tearfully over the phone, "My son has been slipping into the ways of the world. I did not know what to do for him. When he was younger, he used to be a very heavy sleeper. And the only way we could wake him up was by dumping water on his face. When you threw that water on him, it was so prophetically accurate, my son knew he had to get right with the Lord. Since that time, he has been living a holy life." Praise God, obedience to God's voice may seem crazy at times but it will always produce God's results.

Anointed words come from an anointed mind. The Bible teaches us that every person who has been Christed, or anointed, has the mind of Christ (see 1 Cor. 2:16). It is important for us to focus and meditate on what God has actually given us—His mind! We can really think like God because First Corinthians chapter 2 says that the Spirit of God searches the deep things of God and the mind of Christ can receive the things of the Spirit of God. The more we focus in on what God has said about us, the more God's thoughts will be established in our own thinking.

THE HEM OF HIS GARMENT

When Jesus was on earth, people were anxiously awaiting the

Messiah. They knew that when the Messiah came, He would do Messianic miracles. This was the standard Jewish thinking of the day. The Sanhedrin, which served as the ruling council on religious matters, had an advisory board that judged the authenticity of miracles being performed.

When Jesus restored sight to the man who was born blind, the Sanhedrin called the man before this special board to question how he had received his healing. They even questioned his parents. They did not understand how a *sinner* could heal the blind, nor how a sinner could receive his sight. When subjected to a barrage of questions, the man admitted he did not know whether Jesus was a sinner or not. Nevertheless, he pointed out the fact that such a deed had not even been heard of in Israel, that any man, sinner or not, could heal someone born blind. Even as they reviled him for being Jesus' disciple, he spoke boldly the reason why God had healed him:

> *The man answered and said to them, "Why, this is a marvelous thing, that you do not know where He is from; yet He has opened my eyes! Now we know that God does not hear sinners; but if anyone is a worshiper of God and does His will, He hears him. Since the world began it has been unheard of that anyone opened the eyes of one who was born blind. If this Man were not from God, He could do nothing"* (John 9:30-33).

Many believe that when the man spoke of worshiping God and doing His will, he was speaking of Jesus. I disagree. I believe the man was saying, while I was blind I worshipped the Lord from a pure heart, and God heard me. I am considered the worst among sinners because of infirmity that I had all of my life; and yet God heard me. Listen, friends: some of you are like this blind man. You have been struggling for a long time; yet you have not given up worshiping the Lord. You need to know that God hears you! A season is coming when those who have worshiped God in Spirit and in Truth will be set free in ways that they have never imagined. Do not stop worshiping God. Keep meditating on and speaking God's Word. That Word is about to become flesh in your life! Do not give up now. He is about to move for you.

Needless to say, the Sanhedrin was furious that this "sinner" would try to teach them. They were probably jealous and convicted by the truth the man spoke, yet they would not hear him. They cast him out of the synagogue.

The job of this council was to prove such matters that might reveal the Messiah. Most Christians today do not realize that there were others of Jesus' time, especially some Pharisees, doing miracles. But the council was looking for the next level. Many men of God had arisen and ministered God's goodness in the same way that Elijah and Elisha had healed the sick and raised the dead. Yet, there were specific miracles that were only to be performed by the Messiah. One of these miracles was healing a person who was born blind. Although they heard solid testimony of Jesus' Messianic miracles, he did not fit their expectation. They struggled with explaining His background. Where did he derive His authority? Under what Pharisee did He receive His training? And, of course, the last straw was that no prophet had arisen out of Galilee. During His upbringing Jesus moved around through so many towns that it messed things up regarding their prophetic expectations. I believe God set that up on purpose, to create a mystery that would upset their traditional thinking.

After Jesus' baptism by John, He began to do Messianic miracles. Messianic miracles are creative miracles. He did things that only the Messiah could do. Blind people had been healed in the past but never one born blind. The real Messiah was showing up, *but they could not comprehend it in their thinking.* Thus they made the mistake of setting themselves in opposition to the very Spirit of God. The men who were judging Jesus were the leaders of the religious system of that day; amazingly, these men had the first five books of the Bible memorized! They "knew" the Scriptures by heart, and yet they did not recognize their Creator when He stood in front of them. They were blinded by a religious and prideful mentality that controlled every part of their lives.

I have read that during this time of history, the Book of Malachi was often read in the temple. This is how the woman with the issue of blood was able to receive her healing. Somehow she had heard about Jesus healing people. She heard about all the miracles that were happening. Could he be the one prophesied about in Malachi 4:3? She had likely heard the teaching of Malachi many times in the temple. She thought to herself that if I may but touch the hem of His garment I will be made whole. She thought about it until it became her focus. For years she had been sick, but had always held out the hope for a healing Messiah.

> But to you who fear My name
> The Sun of Righteousness shall arise
> With healing in His wings;
> And you shall go out
> And grow fat like stall-fed calves.
> You shall trample the wicked,
> For they shall be ashes under the soles of your feet
> On the day that I do this,"
> Says the Lord of hosts (Malachi 4:2-3).

At this point, it is important to understand something about the culture and history of that day. Jesus walked blameless in all of the instructions of the laws of Moses (the Torah). The wings referred to in the above verse are the tassels on the end of the garment that every male Jew (including Jesus) was instructed by law to wear, especially during prayer. It was much like the modern prayer shawl, or *tallit*, that Jews wear to this day. In Jesus' time, this special garment was sometimes thought to have healing in its *wings* (tassels). Jesus wore a prayer shawl when He prayed. When Jewish men prayed, they would cover their faces with the prayer shawl, and because of the length of it, the tassels or fringes would hang down toward the ground. When they were covered with it, they would enter the secret place. When they came out of prayer, they would lift up the garment to readjust it, causing it to resemble wings. When Jesus entered the secret place, the anointing would flow. The glory that consumed Him on the inside would begin to flow out of His very body, even into His clothes and His outer garment, the tallit. Even from His prayer shawl, the anointing would flow from the head down. The healing anointing was able to flow through Jesus' clothing.

To trust God and His Word is always in alignment with God's heartbeat.

The woman with the issue of blood knew all of this. She was a Jewish woman who would have been acquainted with her culture and historical background, as well as the tallit and the secret place of prayer. She recognized that everywhere Jesus went, healing flowed from Him. I am sure that she recognized Him as the Sun of Righteousness that would rise with healing in His wings (see Mal. 4:2). She said to herself that if she could just touch the hem (the tip of the wings) of His garment, she would be made whole. She knew that when He was in prayer, the anointing would flow, and she would be healed if she touched the tassel. Her heart and thoughts were set like flint toward Jesus. She meditated on the truth in her heart, "If I can just touch the tip of His garment, I will be made whole" (Mark 5:28, paraphrased).

I can imagine as she was pushing and crawling her way through the crowd, she said this statement over and over to herself, meditating on the truth she knew. She was focused on Jesus' power to heal her.

She set her face like flint to touch Him, and she believed that when she did, her healing would manifest. It is interesting to notice that this woman never asked Jesus to heal her. She did not have to beg God for her restoration. She knew God's Word and she believed that God would perform His Word. This was the meditation of her heart, thoughts that were birthed out of God's Spirit.

Peter was conscious that the greater works were flowing through him.

God's Thoughts Emanate Power

In a similar way, in Acts, many people were healed when the people brought their sick out into the streets so that the shadow of Peter would pass over them, and they would be healed. This was likely the shadow of his garment—his wings. We know that Peter traveled with Jesus for three and a half years, watching the Messiah do incredible miracles of power. I am sure that when Peter came upon a sick person, he would remind himself of the awesome miracles that Jesus performed. Peter's mediations had to be on the power and love of God for mighty miracles to take place. I am convinced that when he saw the crowds of sick people in the streets, he remembered the crowds that pushed around Jesus constantly as He walked down the road from town to town. He probably recalled the miracle of the woman with the issue of blood. Peter knew what Jesus had promised him concerning doing the greater works. Jesus had also promised that the Holy Spirit would bring all things that Jesus had taught him to his remembrance. This would include the encouraging memories of God's manifested power. He knew that God wanted him to walk in a greater dimension of God's power than even Jesus had walked in. Peter had meditated on God's will for healing and delivering His people so much that he saw God's power not only flowing through his outer garments, but also radiating from his body. Peter stepped into a greater realm of the anointing by allowing God's glory to emanate from his person and overshadow the people who were diseased.

Thoughts focused on doubt and fear rob us of the fruit of thoughts focused on faith and love. Thoughts remaining in faith and love will destroy doubt and fear!

All of this is vitally important to what God wants to do in our lives. God wants us to have confidence in what He has placed inside of us. Whether we truly believe that we have been anointed with the same anointing that Jesus received form His Father or not will determine our effectiveness in reaching the lost. It is the same concerning healing for ourselves and for the people around us. We have to know beyond a shadow of a doubt that what God said, He will also do. We need to meditate on the truth of God's Word, not on the false evidence that appears real surrounding our lives. When the woman with the issue of blood came to Jesus, she did not come with wishful thinking. If you touch Jesus with a wish, nothing will happen! The woman with the issue of blood had thought about it and thought about it. She had made it her focus and drive. In your thoughts, you must focus to the point of going from wish to know. That means you cannot just say I wish it would happen. You have to come to the place in your thinking that you know when you get ready to come for a miracle you will come ready to touch the hem of His garment, and as a result you will be made whole.

That is the transition from wishful thinking to really knowing. That is what God wants to be established in our minds. She was convincing her soul to move forward toward her goal: she set her gaze on the point of focus, just as Jesus set His gaze on joy. Remember, the Bible says that God is the same yesterday, today, and forever. The same amazing victory that this woman received because of her belief and focus is offered to each one of us by God. Touch His garment and you will have a miracle. By this she was acknowledging that He is the Messiah. He does have healing in His wings. Her thoughts could not be hanging in the balance. The Bible says that a double-minded man is unstable in all his ways and should not expect to receive anything from the Lord. God is trying to get our volatile characteristics and thoughts to be secure and solid and focused. He wants us to know who we are. He wants us to know how He can speak through us and think through us!

IGNITING A FIRE OF WORDS

God's Word is God-breathed. God upholds all things by the Word of His mouth. His Word sustains everything in the universe, preceded only by His thoughts. What we think is very important. The Bible teaches us that whatever a man sows, that he shall also reap. If we continue in old patterns of thinking from our past, we are constantly sowing thoughts of unbelief and doubt. We are sowing thoughts of condemnation and fear! We will continue to walk in the very things from which Christ's blood has made us free, as if He had never died at all. If we refuse, for stubbornness or fear, to allow the Holy Spirit to "create in us a clean heart," we will forever be bound in the nonsense of death, poverty, sickness, and fear. However, if we willingly yield to the Holy Spirit's power to renew our thoughts and clean our hearts so that we can have God's thoughts and mentalities, we will soon begin to sow righteous and victorious thoughts. If we sow to the Spirit, we will reap of the Spirit. If we sow to the flesh, we will reap of the flesh. If we begin to think on prosperity and the blessings of God, and allow those words to come out of our mouths, we will begin to undo the harvest of unbelief that we sowed in ignorance. This may take some time. However, God's Word says that His mercies are new every morning (see Lam. 3:22-23). God will make a way for us where there seems to be no way, even when we have hindered our own progress. I will soon reap a harvest of prosperity and blessing because I am aligning my thoughts with God's desire to pour out blessings upon me.

> *Because he did not remember to show mercy,*
> *But persecuted the poor and needy man,*
> *That he might even slay the broken in heart.*
> *As he loved cursing, so let it come to him;*
> *As he did not delight in blessing, so let it be far from*
> *him* (Psalm 109:16-17).

God delights in the prosperity of His people. The above verse says that the man mentioned did not delight in blessing others or himself. If you do not delight in blessings, then they will be far from you. If you do not delight in blessings, then you have an ungrateful heart. God will not bless that type of attitude. The word *delight* implies that the thing brings you continual pleasure. This word means that you think about it, meditate on it, long for it. It is your eye's desire. I know people who do not get excited about blessings because they think you have to be poor in order to be truly humble. That is a lie from the devil. A spirit of poverty binds them from seeing that God is rich and we are the children of the King. We are the sheep of His pasture. Their thinking does not delight in prosperity, and so prosperity will be far from them. This man was not excited about blessing, so it never came to him. If you do not determine within yourself that you are excited about something that is going to bring you to the place that God has for you, then you will never get there. God wants you to rejoice in the fact that He wants you blessed. So your thinking needs to change from a poverty mentality to a prosperity mentality.

A poverty mentality says poverty equals holiness. A prosperity mentality says money equals souls! A poverty mentality says Jesus was poor. A prosperity mentality says Jesus owns the cattle on a thousand hills (see Ps. 50:10); He had a money bag and took care of the poor. A poverty mentality says, Jesus was homeless. A prosperity mentality says, my Father has prepared a place for me! A poverty mentality says, God wants us to be slaves. A prosperity mentality says, *I will sit as a king in the gates.*

If you focus your thoughts on sickness, it is difficult to be healed. If you watch sick people, you will see that they focus their thoughts on their own personal sickness. Sickness by its very nature tries to draw attention to itself. It hurts. A lot of times people even get angry because of their sickness. Anger acts like a poison to the system. You see people who get into worry and anxiety, and before you know it, their thoughts get progressive. As the thoughts become darker, sickness and disease can begin to rise as the thoughts that are meditated on begin to breed, multiplying the darkness. You need to ask yourself, how much time do I spend having angry thoughts? I have met many people in my travels who have experienced chronic sickness which, when they were freed from anger and bitterness, left them as well.

> *At the bidding of unlawful thoughts the body sinks rapidly into disease and decay; at the command of glad and beautiful thoughts it becomes clothed with youthfulness and beauty.*[4]

People who live in fear of disease are the people who find themselves struggling with sickness. Proverbs 23:7 tells us that as a man thinks in his heart so is he. If a person constantly meditates on or fears becoming sick, their meditation will become their reality. Thoughts of malice, envy, disappointment, despondency rob the body of its health and grace. There is power in allowing God to penetrate and control your thoughts. Do not let thoughts go unbridled. Bitter and unforgiving thoughts will breed all kinds of sickness. The reason this is true lies in the fact that bitterness and unforgiveness are part of satan's nature and character. When we operate in the enemy's territory, we open the door for the enemy to attack us and to work with the seeds that are not of God in our hearts. Jesus told us in John 10:10, "The thief does not come except to steal, and to kill, and to destroy. I have come that they may have life, and that they may have it more abundantly." Sickness and death are part of the enemy's strategy, while abundant life is part of God's strategy. When we operate in satan's character, we are opening the doorway to satan's strategies.

Calmness of spirit and thought will bring health and strength to your body.

The devil is trying to find a crack to get in. He is looking for a way to break you down and get you to meditate on his system. Do not let thoughts go unbridled; if you allow your thoughts to run around like wild horses, then you will never be in control. Thoughts are the beginning of what you are getting ready to do. This is how rebellious actions are birthed. A person meditates on offense, and pride grows. Do not choose your own direction through rebellious thoughts that do not line up with the Word of God. You need to bridle your thoughts and bring them into submission to God's Spirit and God's Word.

When I kept silent, my bones grew old
Through my groaning all the day long (Psalm 32:3).

David was keeping the sinful thoughts he was having to himself. Even though he was not expressing his thoughts out loud, he was meditating on them in his heart. He grumbled and complained when he was by himself. His bones grew old because he continually thought these wrong thoughts. David knew that through his groanings his bones would grow old. A man cannot directly choose his circumstances, but by the word of faith he can alter his circumstances. In contrast to the growing old of David's bones, when he confessed his sin to God, it became strength to him.

> *I acknowledged my sin to You,*
> *And my iniquity I have not hidden.*
> *I said, "I will confess my transgressions to the Lord,"*
> *And You forgave the iniquity of my sin* (Psalm 32:5).

Walking in the calmness of God, disciplining your thoughts so that they stay bridled and under the direction of the Holy Spirit, is the key to bodily health and wholeness.

> *I said, "I will guard my ways,*
> *lest I sin with my tongue;*
> *I will restrain my mouth with a muzzle,*
> *While the wicked are before me."*
> *I was mute with silence,*
> *I held my peace even from good;*
> *And my sorrow was stirred up.*
> *My heart was hot within me;*
> *While I was musing, the fire burned.*
> *Then I spoke with my tongue...* (Psalm 39:1-3).

> *I said to myself, "I'm going to quit complaining!*
> *I'll keep quiet, especially when the ungodly are around*
> *   me."*
> *But as I stood there silently the turmoil within me grew*
> *   to the bursting point.*
> *The more I mused, the hotter the fires inside.*
> *Then at last I spoke and pled with God* (Psalm 39:1-2
> TLB).

Think Like God

My thoughts grew hot within me and began to burn,
igniting a fire of words (Psalm 39:3 NLT).

What was he saying? Basically: I kept my mouth shut until I meditated upon what God wanted me to meditate on. When I began to meditate on what God wanted me to, I felt the fire burn inside of me, and I decided to talk. The Word of God that I meditated on became a fire shut up in my bones. I could no longer hold back the utterance of God because the fire of the Word was consuming me from the inside out.

There is no prophetic unction that is of any good unless the fire of God is backing it.

God's prophetic utterance is birthed out of the meditations of the heart. When the Word of God takes on voice in your heart, it will burn like a fire inside of you until you cannot hold it back any longer. This is how the prophetic is correctly birthed: by meditation on the Word of God and by fire.

Because we spend time complaining to ourselves in our thoughts, we murmur and complain with our mouths; as a result our bones waste away. Negative thoughts always stop miracles. Remember when the children of Israel murmured and complained, 23,000 people fell down dead. In the light of his miraculous display of power in Moses' time, God did not tolerate the grumbling and complaining of the children of Israel. God caused plagues to come on them to get them to stop their constant negativity. He told them, just as you say, I will bring it to pass. That is why negative thoughts always stop miracles.

A calm and undisturbed mind and heart are the life and
health of the body, but envy, jealousy, and wrath are like
rottenness of the bones (Proverbs 14:30 AMP).

A calm mind produces health and life. Negative thoughts will produce after their own kind. The way that we think is vitally important. Negative thoughts will produce negativity in the bones. Jesus told one of His disciples, "Martha, you are anxious about something that is not the most important thing (see Luke 10:42). He was telling her to calm down and to get her emotions under control. Who can add one cubit to his stature by worry? Do we not serve the God that takes care of the lilies of the field, whose splendor and glory are greater than that of Solomon? How much more will He take care of you? (See Matthew 6:25-34.) Worry will not make you grow or increase or succeed. It will not make you better in anything. So, tell worry to shut up! Set your gaze on joy. Sometimes when I feel worry trying to attack me, I will just begin to laugh. The Bible says that laughter does good like a medicine. The joy of the Lord is my strength and will keep me focused on the Father and His plan and purpose.

> *The light of the eyes rejoices the heart,*
> *And a good report makes the bones healthy* (Proverbs 15:30).

When I look into certain people's eyes, I see light; that light makes my heart rejoice. When I hear uplifting and encouraging words come from people's mouths, it makes me feel victorious. The light in their eyes and the words of their mouth cause life to spring forth in the person they are in contact with. The root of their words is, of course, their pattern of thoughts and mentalities. God wants us to have active and productive thoughts, not passive thoughts. Thoughts like, "Well, I am just not going to apply myself," are the playground for the devil. He wants to take your "inactive" mind and make it a breeding ground for discouragement, doubt, fear, apathy, and rebellion. Have you ever noticed that when you are tired, the first thing the devil tells you to do is sit down and watch television? He knows that when you are tired he can manipulate you a lot more easily. You have to focus yourself on the presence of God and on the mind of Christ, or the devil will find a way to play games with your thoughts.

The Bible says to submit to God, resist the devil, and he will flee from you. We have to train our thoughts to submit to the mind of Christ and to put on the helmet of salvation. You have to know that your mind is secure and protected by the blood of Christ, which cleanses it from all dead works, and by the helmet of salvation, which sets the mind toward things of Heaven and not unimportant and natural circumstances. God is not the author of confusion. He does not have out-of-control thoughts. His thoughts are powerful, directed, and focused. If we feel confused, that is an indication that we have stepped out of God's thoughts into our own. When He releases His words, they always accomplish what they were sent forth to do. If you follow the thoughts of God, the miracle that you are desiring will first be birthed in your thoughts, then in your words, and finally in the full manifestation of your healing.

Sometimes we confess we are tired of fighting the devil. We think we have to fight the devil all of the time. I have good news for you: you will be fighting the devil for the rest of your life, because you will continue to break barriers in the flesh and go from glory to glory in the Spirit. This does not please satan. He does not want you to grow and prosper. He is going to do his best to distract you and stir up your flesh so that you miss God's thoughts at times. You have to keep pressing forward, however, and continue to redirect your thoughts toward God. This is called self-discipline and self-control. Do not allow your thoughts to run wild and go in whatever direction they feel like going. Silence the corrupt desires of the flesh by meditating on God and His Word. This will cause victory for you in your battle against the enemy.

LOVE IN ACTION

While I was ministering to a church in Siberia, a thought occurred to me. I remember telling everyone, "God just showed me that a wind of the Holy Spirit is going to blow through this place and knock all those present over." The minute I spoke this out loud, the entire choir fell over. First I thought about the wind of the Spirit in my mind. Then I pictured it in my imagination. Then I spoke it with my mouth. This is simply a demonstration, although a drastic one, of catching God's flow and administering the movement of the Holy Spirit. That is what He wants all of us to do. He is going to follow through if you get His thoughts and take an active step toward obedience to His command.

What does the anointing accomplish? The anointing dwells in your heart through faith that is rooted and grounded in love. We have to realize that God's love actually propels healing. God's love initiates miracles. God's love is the key to birthing signs and wonders. God is Love, and His heart beats to see people delivered from bondage and corruption of the present age through the Spirit of Christ, the Anointed One and His anointing. Then, when you get ready to do the unbelievable, the unction that we have received from the Holy One tells us exactly what to do to accomplish God-results.

In one service, I noticed a woman sitting in a particular row, and God showed me that she needed healing. Without deliberating in my head I just told her to step out into the aisle. The difference between this and other meetings was that I could sense a Spirit of great love flowing. Love was energizing both my faith and the faith of the woman receiving prayer. Next I told her that God showed me she had cancer in her hips. But God's next instruction was even bolder: "Hit her in the hips," I heard the Anointed One within me say. At this point I had already been obedient, so I simply took the next step. As I hit her in the hips, the anointing was released, the burden was removed, and the miracle took place. The fact that when I obeyed what seemed to be a very strange command from God and the woman was healed, is a stamp of God's approval. The miracle bears witness to the Holy Spirit speaking to me. I get a thought from God, and the Spirit bears witness. As I watch the miraculous take place through my obedience, this builds my confidence in God. The Spirit inside me is speaking forth the answers as I am speaking; the Spirit of God inside me is reaching out to touch people through me.

The Bible says that perfect love casts out all fear. Love is the key that unlocks the mysteries of our faith. When we tap into the love of God in our thoughts, we will receive a greater understanding of God's thoughts working through us. God's love has to be the motive-driving intent of every action we do. If we allow God to transform our thoughts into a mentality birthed in love, we will get an entirely different way of thinking. God's love is a sacrificial love; God's love is a supernatural love. God's love is a manifestation of His power at work to transform human lives into something divine.

> *For I know the thoughts that I think toward you, says the Lord, thoughts of peace and not of evil, to give you a future and a hope* (Jeremiah 29:11).

God is thinking good thoughts about us! It only makes sense that He wants us to have good thoughts concerning our own lives and others. This helps us understand how much God loves us. He is thinking loving thoughts: He is thinking of blessings and a good future for us. When that truth of God's love really takes hold of us, the process of thoughts producing words works for our benefit. We begin to declare what God has for us.

> *For the prophecy came not in old time by the will of man: but holy men of God spoke as they were moved by the Holy Ghost* (2 Peter 1:21 KJV).

For them to minister what they ministered, the Word of God had to go through their minds. God inspired it. What they wrote lined up with the thoughts of God. I get a thought from God, and the Spirit inside of me rests upon that Word. The Spirit of God is the one who brings forth the prophetic Word of God. If a word comes forth that does not line up with the Word of God, we know that it was not the Holy Spirit. It is not I who speaks or wills those words to come forth; it is the mind of God that is birthing the prophetic word. Paul said, I do not come with persuasive words of man's wisdom, but in demonstration and power (see 1 Cor. 2:4). Paul was indicating that God's thoughts of love will move us to demonstrate God's ability to deliver, heal, and empower.

> *The thoughts of the righteous are right,*
> *But the counsels of the wicked are deceitful* (Proverbs 12:5).

The righteous are those in right standing with God. They have taken on God's way of doing and being right. When you know that you are pure and walking according to the precepts of the Father, then your thoughts will automatically be right. That tells me that righteous people must have right thoughts: they are covenant people driven by the principles of covenant. Their motive and intentions are right because they listen to God's heart. One cannot separate the idea of covenant from love. When you abide in love, you are in covenant with God. When the wicked person thinks and then attempts to deceive others, it is clear those are not thoughts of righteousness, birthed out of love for God. Those kinds of thoughts are not in line with covenant.

God wants to eliminate from our lives all ideas, attitudes, and false teachings that do not line up His covenant with us. In the Jewish culture, a covenant was a very powerful alliance between two parties that lasted the lifespan of those parties. If I entered into a covenant with my neighbor, then everything that belongs to me would belong to him as well, and vice versa. If I had debt, my debt would now be my neighbor's as well. If I had money and lands, these would now belong to my neighbor. In the context of the believer and God, when we enter into covenant with God, we come to the table with nothing to offer, except ourselves. However, the moment we step into covenant with God, we receive access to His wealth, riches, love, omnipotence, omnipresence, and omniscience. Everything that He is and everything that He has becomes ours through covenant. We are His children, joint heirs with Christ of God's Kingdom. Covenant gives us a right to tap into God's resources, His righteousness, holiness, and justice. Each time we place a demand on God, it pleases Him because we are affirming that God's Word is truthful and that He is faithful.

> *Commit thy works unto the Lord,*
> *And your thoughts shall be established* [succeed]
> (Proverbs 16:3 KJV).

When we commit everything that we do to God, He will establish our thoughts. Some people's thoughts are not being established because they have not given everything that they have to God. These people want God to give them their desires without the commitment of their lives and resources to God. Everything that we have is a stewardship and really belongs to the Father. If we are not willing to bless God, we cannot expect God to bless us. God's promise is to persons who will sacrifice everything they have and all that they are to God for the purposes of His Kingdom.

Calmness is power! It takes God's plan of wisdom to move you into a place of prosperity. It is important to stay calm and relaxed. We do this by staying focused, putting our trust in God and resting in Him. We need to be diligent to spend time in the presence of God. We need to be diligent to spend time meditating upon the Word of God. We need to be diligent to keep ourselves in the secret place. When we do this, God will establish our thoughts.

All of us are bombarded with thoughts throughout the day. Is it not amazing that when you start praying in tongues, the devil comes along and starts reminding you of everything that you have to do? You try to pray in tongues for twenty minutes, and you always seem to get interrupted about ten times. Often it is not even anything bad, but simply day-to-day responsibilities that need your attention. When that happens, just write down everything he reminds you of and go back to it later. By doing this you sort out the thoughts that are God's and the thoughts that belong to the devil.

Commit your ways to God and determine to get up and pray in tongues every morning; or if you are the evening type do it every night. I believe that if Christians really understood all of the benefits of praying in tongues, they would not be able to stop. You wouldn't even be able to pay them to absorb trash from secular television. This will go a long way in helping to clear out the thoughts that try to choke out the Word. Of course, satan will try to do his job. He is the enemy of a calm mind that is focused on God. He will do everything that he can to keep you from hearing the voice of God. But as you recognize what is going on, this will help you get your mind to the place where it is stable and secure in the presence of God, where it is not constantly moved, worried, and concerned about anything. Like anything else, it gets better and better as you practice.

Think Like God:
GOD-THOUGHTS FOR MEDITATION

- Self-control is strength. Right thoughts are mastery. Calmness is power.
- When you see patience taking the time to apply itself to self-control, you have seen the power of calmness.
- The measure of thought that we apply to the Word that we receive will be the measure of virtue and knowledge that will come back to us.
- A wise man's calmness of mind reveals the fruit of his mental focus toward God's thoughts. It reveals a patient pursuit of self-control.
- Until you get your thoughts connected with the purposes and plans of God, there will be no fruitful or intelligent accomplishment.
- A lack of focus can produce numerous negative and destructive thoughts in a few minutes, because focus determines mastery.
- Fear is false evidence appearing real.
- God's Word is a revelation of God's own thoughts.
- The thought of God is established in the mind of Christ.
- To trust God and His Word is always in alignment with God's heartbeat.
- Peter was conscious that the greater works were flowing through him.

- Thoughts focused on doubt and fear rob us of the fruit of thoughts focused on faith and love.
- Thoughts remaining in faith and love will destroy doubt and fear!
- At the bidding of unlawful thoughts, the body sinks rapidly into thoughts of disease and decay; at the command of glad and beautiful thoughts, it becomes clothed with youthfulness and beauty.
- Calmness of spirit and thought will bring health and strength to your body.
- There is no prophetic unction that is of any good unless the fear of God is backing it.

ENDNOTES

1. James Strong, *The New Strong's Expanded Exhaustive Concordance of the Bible: Strong's Expanded Greek Dictionary of the New Testament.* (Nashville, TN: Thomas Nelson Publishers, 2001,) 78.

2. Ibid., 280.

3. Ibid., 134.

4. James Allen. *As a Man Thinketh* (St. Augustine, FL: AsaManThinketh.net. 2001), 16.

Chapter Seven

From Meditation to Mentality

WHAT IS YOUR MEDITATION?

[Inasmuch as we] refute arguments and theories and
reasonings and every proud and lofty thing that sets itself
up against the [true] knowledge of God; and we lead
every thought and purpose away captive into the obedi-
ence of Christ (the Messiah, the Anointed One)
(2 Corinthians 10:5 AMP).

I think it is safe to say that human beings have always struggled in their thought life. If we start at the very beginning with Adam and Eve, we will see that Eve contemplated eating the fruit, the benefits of it, and why she should be disobedient to God before she actually did the deed (see Gen. 3:6). Again we see this same problem in Cain, who was jealous and angry against his younger brother Abel. Sarah laughed at God and questioned Him in her heart over the prospect of her becoming pregnant at 90 years of age. Abimelech lusted in his heart over Sarah and took her from Abraham. Jacob was deceptive and stole his brother's birthright. Rachel lied to her husband and her father and hid the household gods in her tent.

Think Like God

All these problems started in a man or woman's heart. Sin was birthed because people did not take their thoughts captive. Many Christians have the desire to have Christ-centered thoughts and lives. Yet we must be willing to put the above verse into practice. We actually have to pay attention to what we are thinking about and why. When random thoughts come into our heads, we have to be aware of them and where they come from. When a strange thought runs through my mind, I will stop and ask, why am I thinking that thought? If I can identify whether that thought is of God, of the flesh, or of the devil, I can then recognize whether I should be thinking like that or not. At times we just need to stop and say, where are my thoughts taking me? Are they pointing me toward God and His power and love, or are they mere distractions that will take away from His glory? If my thoughts are not lined up with the Word of God, then they must be taken captive and cast down, as the above verse confirms.

God wants us to recognize something about those "little" thoughts that do not seem to mean anything. One tiny thought can lead to more and more thoughts about the same subject, which can lead to a meditation, which will inevitably lead to a mentality. One "little" thought of bitterness toward a spouse or pastor can lead to more and more bitter and critical thoughts that will lead to a mentality of pride and bitterness. We have to recognize that one thought is enough to start an avalanche of mental activity, which, at some point, will end up being our words, behaviors, and attitudes.

Your meditation always becomes your mentality.

Is it not uncanny how every time you try to get into God's presence, a thought comes along that tries to exalt itself above the knowledge of God? You can almost set your watch to it! These thoughts are sent to oppose you and to cut off your growth in the Spirit. The devil does not want you to spend time with God. In fact, he's going to do everything in his power to hinder you from coming into God's presence.

The solution to the problem is always the same. I think what stumps many people is the simplicity of the resolution that will take us out of this realm of frustration and into the realm of self-discipline and control. Every day you have to take those thoughts that are not of God captive. This is an absolutely indispensable skill that anyone who hopes to mature in God must master. Those contrary thoughts are trying to distract us. The devil does not want you to spend time in God's presence. He will try to put pressure on you while you are praying. He wants to crush your spirit, destroy your confidence, and steal your attention. The enemy will bring up every kind of offense and fear from the past that will distract you from the very things you wanted to pray about. He does not want you to seek God! He does not want you to receive clarity and freedom in your thought life. Remember that when your spirit and your soul—your mind, will, and emotions—agree with each other, the body will follow automatically. We can bring every single thought into obedience to Christ by training our mind, will, and emotions to agree with God's Word.

Here is a prayer of declaration that helps me take every thought captive to the obedience of Christ:

> *I thank You, Father, that I can come into Your presence with boldness to find grace and help in the time of need. I thank You, Father, that my mind is in alignment with the Word of God and the Spirit of God. I declare right now that I think like God. I declare that I am free from old patterns of thinking, saying, and doing things. I declare that I am a sheep and I hear the voice of the Shepherd. Another voice I will not and cannot follow. Thank You, Father, that my mind is a conduit for Your Word and power. Right now I take every thought captive to the*

obedience of Christ. I rebuke every spirit of fear and condemnation. I declare that I am free from the voice of the past. I declare I am accepted in the Beloved. Thank You, Father, for loving me! In Jesus' name, Amen!

BREAKING DREAM PATTERNS

The mentality that we choose for today will affect our tomorrows. The thoughts we think today will remain with us down the road. Most people do not realize how their mentality affects every part of their lives. Even our sleep will be affected by an unruly thought life during the day. For example, I have heard people say they have a problem with sinful dreams, but have basically given up fighting them, because they think they do not have control over their dreams. Dreams, however, are a result of the kind of meditation that rules our waking hours. Do not misunderstand what I am saying. There are times when we will have dreams that may be soulish or unholy to a certain extent even though we have set our minds on things above during the day. I have noticed that deep heart issues that have not been completely purged out, though they may not manifest while we are awake, will become painfully obvious to us in our dreams. This is God's mercy, in that He is letting us know the areas of our hearts that still need to be sanctified. Many dreams will come out of issues that were discussed during the day. Sometimes it takes a while for negative thoughts or past sins to come to the surface, and they will often do so through dreams. When this happens, deal with them strongly, and they will not come back. Every morning upon awaking, I encourage you to declare that the blood of Jesus Christ purges your conscience from all dead works.

Nevertheless, dreams are most often connected to the kinds of thoughts we have allowed to come into our mind on a regular basis. We have to remember that just because our body is resting does not mean that our minds and spirits are not awake. On the contrary, a man's spirit does not sleep; the Scripture says that a man's spirit seeks God while the body sleeps. So we can assume that whatever is being processed over and over again during the day is going to be the ruling pattern during the night. If you are having multiple ungodly dreams, take some time to really watch what you think about during the day. When thoughts that you know are not from God come up, cast them down in the name of Jesus Christ and turn your mind to meditating on what is pure, lovely, noble, and of good report. Then before you go to sleep, place your hands on your head and declare this simple confession:

> *I thank You, Father, that I have the mind of Christ. I thank You that I have an anointed mind. I thank You, Father, that no weapon formed against me will prosper. I thank You, Father, that You bless Your beloved with sweet sleep. I thank You that as I lay my head down on my pillow, I receive rest from You. I thank You that while I sleep, the Word keeps me. I thank You that You give me dreams and visions in night seasons and speak to me while I sleep. I thank You that I wake on time and with the exact amount of rest that I need to function to my full capacity during the day. In Jesus' name, Amen!*

WHAT YOU THINK IS WHAT YOU BELIEVE

At times, the Holy Spirit moves me to sit down and reread the accounts of Jesus' miracles, the mighty signs and wonders that He performed while He was on earth. I can recognize that His actions were birthed out of a pure conscience, a mind that was wholly consecrated to the Father. Jesus meditated on the Word of God, which at that time was the Hebrew Scriptures. Therefore, we know that He read the hundreds of supernatural encounters that humans had with the God of Abraham, Isaac, and Jacob. Jesus would have studied how

God split the Red Sea and caused manna to fall from Heaven like rain; He would have encountered the God who appeared as a pillar of fire by night and a pillar of cloud by day. Jesus meditated on the God who made the Israelites' shoes last for 40 years; Jesus knew the stories of the wall of Jericho falling down and the plagues which God sent on the Egyptians.

Everything that Jesus read in the Scriptures about His Father showed Him that the God of the Old Covenant was a supremely powerful God who could and did alter nature and men through supernatural means. Therefore, when He ran into a storm on the lake one day, Jesus knew what His Father in Heaven would do. Surely the God who sent the flood and dried up the Jordan could calm the winds and the waves as well! For Jesus to rebuke the winds and the waves was nothing for Him. Jesus did not have to stop and think about what He should do before He did it—to walk in the supernatural was written into His very being as God's Child. This is one of the reasons why Jesus instructed His disciples, do not take thought concerning your life—what you will eat or drink or wear—as if you can add one inch to your stature by meditating on what you need! Do not be concerned for what is of the natural, because we have a God who brings the supernatural into the natural to make it conform to His will. Jesus only gave thought to the fact that He had dominion over the natural. His meditation determined His perspective on all of creation.

Your meditation will affect how you view all of creation.

As God's chosen ones, His dear children, we also have come into covenant with the God of the supernatural. We are no longer bound by the natural circumstances and hindrances that people experience in the world. For example, from the world's perspective, the only way for a person to get from Los Angeles to New York quickly is by taking a plane. However, this natural barrier does not exist in God's reality. He is in both cities at the same time.

Though this might stretch your faith, I want you to think outside of the box. Acts chapter 8 tells us a fascinating story about Philip the evangelist. This chapter explains how God used Philip to touch Samaria with the Gospel, and also how Philip ministered to a eunuch. After he had baptized the eunuch, Philip was caught away in the Spirit and was found some distance away in a city. Philip was translated in the Spirit from where he was at with the eunuch to another place. This is the kind of occurrence in the Scriptures that reveal God's heartbeat for His children to not only experience the supernatural, but to become supernatural beings! The Word of God does not say that after Jesus left the earth, God looked down from Heaven and said, "Well, there's no need for miracles anymore." In fact the same need that arose during Jesus' lifespan was still very prevalent in the days of the apostles: people are hungry for a God who can transform their circumstances, a God that offers them more than the promise of life after death.

If the Church is honest, the generation we are in today faces the exact same predicament. People want to see Jesus! They want to touch Jesus! They want to know Jesus! They do not have any desire to come and sit on a pew for an hour and listen to a 20-minute sermon and afterward go about their lives as if the church building did not even exist. What is the number one question that I have been asked by nonbelievers? "If there is a God and He loves us, then why is there evil in the world?" And, boy, do we scramble for the excuses! The truth for nonbelievers is that they do not want to serve a God who does not change what goes on in the natural. They do not want an aloof God who is unattached and uninvolved and makes no promises. We as His children have got to come to a point where we can demonstrate this supernatural God! If we cannot, then we have nothing to offer. I tell you the truth, souls will come into the Kingdom only to the degree that we manifest the nature and character of God to them.

Have you ever had a bad habit that you wanted to break? You make a plan to take steps toward adjusting your behavior, but it seems difficult to actually do those steps instead of returning to the normal habit. Have you ever thought about what a habit is? It is a pattern or consistent way of doing something. Habits are formed out of thinking patterns, and in order to break a habit we have to break a mentality. Just as it took time to form that habit, it will also take time to break it off of your life. What you think about continually will eventually cause a specific belief system to grow in your heart. I cannot emphasize enough the fact that what we believe in our hearts is a result of our meditation. If we think wrongly about a certain subject for a long enough period of time (to the point where thought becomes meditation), then we will believe wrongly about that subject. For example, if I tell one of my children for the first three years of his or her life that three plus three equals seven, that child will believe that three plus three is seven, even though it is not! If we believe wrongly, then what we say will inevitably be wrong. The habits we practice in our lives will be a direct result of the right or wrong thinking patterns that we meditate on consistently.

RESTING OUR THOUGHTS IN THE WORD

One specific way to correct wrong thinking patterns is to read the Word of God out loud. The Word of God will be the key to making massive adjustments in one's thinking. Speaking the Word out loud to yourself will establish faith in your thought life faster than any other way. Remember that faith comes by hearing and hearing by the Word of God. The only way true faith can be birthed in our thinking is by allowing the Word of God to open the ears of our hearts and minds so that we can hear God's voice. As we meditate on the words of God, the Word we receive will open our spiritual ears to hear more of what God wants to say to and through us. Then we inevitably confess what we have been meditating on.

As I have explained, meditating on God's Word will adjust your words; but it is also true that speaking God's Word will adjust your thoughts. We can also realign our thinking by what we say. Confession will realign our thinking. Knowing this, we need to speak out the Word of God. As we do, we will hear the Word of God, and our thinking will be altered. God's Word contains God's thoughts; when we read God's Word out loud, it is sort of like self-infiltration. Our minds have no choice but to hear and comprehend our words. As we are looking at the words on the page, and we say the Word with our own mouths, we are hearing the words with our ears, and we are comprehending the words with our minds.

I believe the best way to learn a revelation is to preach it; when you read the Word of God out loud, you will be preaching to your own spirit: you will hear your own voice speaking truth over your life. This is a quick way to change the way you think about yourself. You are letting God's thoughts flow through your mind, out of your mouth, and into your mind again. I have a good friend who is a professor in a Bible college. Even though he teaches college-level classes, he often makes his students do their reading assignments from the Word out loud. He obviously realizes the fact that reading the Word out loud profoundly affects the way a person thinks.

There are usually three centers for wrong thoughts within the mind. First, wrong thoughts about who God is; second, wrong thoughts about who we are; and third, wrong thoughts in relationship to others. As you begin to meditate on God's Word, you will find that these three areas of wrong thinking will begin to be exposed. You may come across a verse that strikes at a lie that you have believed since you were a small child. One lie I know many children are taught is that it is perfectly normal and right for a person to be afraid. However, the Bible teaches the exact opposite. In fact there are over 365 times in the Bible where God says, "Do not fear." If we really believe the Word of God is true, then we must allow the Word to expose lies we believe about the Father, about ourselves, and about others. By establishing within ourselves that God's Word will have dominion over our minds, and by allowing that Word to expose and destroy the lies of the enemy, that same Word will begin to transform our thoughts into heavenly, God-centered thoughts. As we set our minds on things above and not on things beneath (see Col. 3:2), where Christ is seated at the right hand of the Father making intercession for us, our hearts will be refreshed, and our minds will begin to rest in the place of confidence.

> *You will keep him in perfect peace,*
> *Whose mind is stayed on You,*
> *Because he trusts in You* (Isaiah 26:3).

MEDITATION DETERMINES CREATIVITY

If what you meditate upon is not establishing, maneuvering, or building the creative power of God in you, then you need to eliminate it. This is the gold standard of the thoughts of God. By washing your mind with the pure water of the Word, you will purge out those thoughts that do not produce the glory of God. Remember, the blood of Christ will purge your consciousness from all dead works.

> *Not with the blood of goats and calves, but with His own blood He entered the Most Holy Place once for all, having obtained eternal redemption. For if the blood of bulls and goats and the ashes of a heifer, sprinkling the unclean, sanctifies for the purifying of the flesh, how much more shall the blood of Christ, who through the eternal Spirit offered Himself without spot to God, cleanse your conscience from dead works to serve the living God?* (Hebrews 9:12-14)

Once your mind is purged from dead works and washed in the water of the Word, God will begin to develop His creative power in your mind. Thinking like God will help you develop dreams and visions, which are the seeds of the future. If I have dreams and visions in which I see myself laying hands on people and see missing arms and legs growing, then I am starting to see the creative dimension of God manifesting in my own consciousness. I am seeing a place where God's prophetic imagination intends for me to go. Through dreams and visions, the thoughts are getting established for God to release creative power. Our ability to dream dreams was not intended by God to be wasted on regurgitating past sins, having nightmares, or conjuring up pornographic nonsense. Like everything else God made, our ability to dream was created for a godly purpose. The Body of Christ is desperate to break this barrier and step into the fullness of God's power by reaching the levels of potential that God placed inside of His children. This truth applies in every area of our lives, including dreams and visions.

Before we will see God's creative power flowing through us, we must be able to believe that God's creative power can manifest in our own lives. The process of allowing the bigness of God's power to manifest through us starts with our mentality. When I see a person in a wheelchair, does my imagination conjure up pictures of that person walking? Do I see the person jumping up and down, praising the Lord for the miracle He just performed? Or do I believe in my heart that they will always be in that wheelchair? Though I am not the person in the wheelchair, I am contributing to the person's circumstances by my unbelief. The creativity of God starts in being confident of God's creative power. I must believe that God is still in the business of raising the dead and healing the sick, and that He wants to use me to accomplish the supernatural.

MENTALITY OF WORSHIP

We have many weapons of warfare at our disposal in order to

combat incorrect thinking. Another way to rectify false thoughts is to enter into the place of worship. In one sense, worship is meditating on God's power and His loving kindness. Worship is the recognition that Christ Jesus is King of kings and Lord of lords. When we recognize that Jesus is our Master and our Land Lord (He owns everything), we are worshiping Him. Worship is to give over total control to Him as an act of adoration and devotion. When you worship God, all other thoughts freeze, and your mind begins to focus on the Lord. That is why the Bible teaches that God literally inhabits the praises of His people. When you praise God, lauding His wonderful works and attributes, you are building a house for God; when you worship Him, entering into sweet intimacy with Him, God comes to possess you and the house you have built for Him. God will always come to possess what is His. He will never allow anything that belongs to Him to be lost; for this reason when many people worship God, they experience healing and deliverance. God sees His own nature and character in their worship and rescues what is of Him within us. (Please read *God Working With God: Love and Worship* for more information!) Our thoughts are completely centered on adoring the Lover of our souls, because all other things vanish when we look into the face of a holy God.

To have pure and holy thoughts that are centered on God's love and power should be one of our main goals as Christians, because all actions come out of our thoughts. Unfortunately, pure and holy thoughts do not simply chase you down, as the negative ones seem to do. Believers must actively pursue what is pure to be able to experience the fullness of the mind of God.

When David faced the Philistine giant, Goliath, he was but a boy. He was not stronger or smarter than other boys his age, and compared to his older brothers, who were tall and strong and handsome, he really did not have much to offer in the face of such pessimistic circumstances. Yet none of this moved David. When he approached King Saul to ask permission to fight the Philistine, Saul laughed at him and mocked him. Not even the opinion of the king of Israel mattered to David. The boy replied, "My God rescued me from the lion and the bear. This giant shall be like one of them before me!" (See 1 Samuel 17.) David's meditation was not on the bigness of his opponent; rather, David set his eyes on the One who had delivered him in the past, namely, God. The victories of the past created a working grid in David's mind to have yet another victory. David recalled in his mind the faithfulness and the power of God to deliver him in the past. Victory had already developed in his consciousness.

As we stand in situations where there are giants ahead that we must face, we must worship God for His past victories in our lives. We must meditate on God's bigness and recognize that He is about to move on our behalf again. Praise can be defined as a recount of God's goodness in our lives, reminding us of His mighty works of salvation and glory. When we recognize all that God has accomplished on our behalf, we will be moved to worship Him in the beauty of holiness and be expectant as to what God is going to do in our future.

DOMINION MENTALITY

The account of the time after Israel was miraculously delivered from Egypt contains a wealth of truth concerning the need for God's people to think like Him. Take Caleb, for example. Caleb was one of two men, among twelve leaders of Israel, who came back from spying out the land of Canaan. Of these twelve men, only two among them proclaimed that Israel was able to take the land. They were Joshua and Caleb. The other ten were filled with fear and declared that the land was full of giants and could never be taken. Caleb could never have acted and spoken like he did without having developed a dominion mentality. While others focused and meditated on the negative, he was recalling in his mind all the victories that God had given them in the wilderness.

195

The Lord said to Moses, "Send men to spy out the land of Canaan, which I give to the people of Israel; from each tribe of their fathers shall you send a man, every one a leader among them." So Moses sent them from the wilderness of Paran, according to the command of the Lord, all of them men who were heads of the people of Israel (Numbers 13:1-3 RSV).

Moses sent them to spy out the land of Canaan, and said to them, "Go up into the Negeb yonder, and go up into the hill country, and see what the land is, and whether the people who dwell in it are strong or weak, whether they are few or many, and whether the land that they dwell in is good or bad, and whether the cities that they dwell in are camps or strongholds, and whether the land is rich or poor, and whether there is wood in it or not. Be of good courage, and bring some of the fruit of the land." Now the time was the season of the first ripe grapes (Numbers 13:17-20 RSV).

And they told him, "We came to the land to which you sent us; it flows with milk and honey, and this is its fruit. Yet the people who dwell in the land are strong, and the cities are fortified and very large; and besides, we saw the descendants of Anak there. The Amalekites dwell in the land of the Negeb; the Hittites, the Jebusites, and the Amorites dwell in the hill country; and the Canaanites dwell by the sea, and along the Jordan." But Caleb quieted the people before Moses, and said, "Let us go up at once, and occupy it; for we are well able to overcome it" (Numbers 13:27-30 RSV).

Caleb chose in his thought life to meditate upon the power of God.

He knew when he went into the Promised Land that all the peoples there and their armies and weaponry could not stand before the mighty God of Heaven. Their puny strength was nothing compared to God's omnipotence. Look at his attitude, "…we are well able to overcome it." His confidence was not in Israel's army, in their weaponry or numbers; his confidence was in the true and living God.

> *Then the men who had gone up with him said, "We are not able to go up against the people; for they are stronger than we." So they brought to the people of Israel an evil report of the land which they had spied out, saying, "The land, through which we have gone, to spy it out, is a land that devours its inhabitants; and all the people that we saw in it are men of great stature. And there we saw the Nephilim (the sons of Anak, who come from the Nephilim); and we seemed to ourselves like grasshoppers, and so we seemed to them." Then all the congregation raised a loud cry; and the people wept that night. And all the people of Israel murmured against Moses and Aaron; the whole congregation said to them, "Would that we had died in the land of Egypt! Or would that we had died in this wilderness!"* (Numbers 13:31-14:2 RSV)

Moses should have told them to shut their mouths. Because of the grumbling and complaining mouths, thousands had already died, and much time had been wasted. Now, standing on the edge of the destiny, the Israelites got cold feet because of some giants. I have seen this happen to many people whom I have known. God brings them through a wilderness period in their lives, using it to produce trust and intimacy; as they approach their inheritance, however, they begin to question God. They think that this job is too big for them: "I do not have the skills to take on this assignment. I am not called to do that! I do not enjoy doing that! I am not mature enough to handle that." They begin to speak against the fulfillment of God's promise to them, and for that reason, they either never receive what God has for them, or it takes 20 years of their lives to figure out and do what God is asking of them.

> *And they said to one another, "Let us choose a captain, and go back to Egypt." Then Moses and Aaron fell on their faces before all the assembly of the congregation of the people of Israel* (Numbers 14:4-5 RSV).

If we want to enter the Promised Land, we must deal with the voice of the past trying to bind us to Egypt.

Moses did not instruct them to go ahead and leave. He knew for a fact that leader would not have gotten very far in the wilderness before he would have been destroyed for rebellion or would have decided to go back and join the family. Had God allowed them to go, they probably would have started remembering how bad Egypt really was before they even got back. Perhaps he would have given them time to think about whether they wanted to go back to Egypt and slavery, or if they wanted to go back to the Promised Land and take it. But Moses was not a confronter, and I believe that was a serious mistake in Moses' life. We have to confront and deal with things sometimes if we want to take people into the Promised Land.

> *And the Lord said to Moses, "How long will this people despise me? And how long will they not believe in me, in spite of all the signs which I have wrought among them? I will strike them with the pestilence and disinherit them,*

and I will make of you a nation greater and mightier than they" (Numbers 14:11-12 RSV).

Remarkably, God was saying, I will wipe them all out and start all over again just as I did with Noah. After all, God's chosen people had become lazy and rebellious, full of unbelief and fear. But this is just another good example of God trying to provoke a faith response in Moses, and adjust his thinking. God knew what He had spoken concerning the Israelites—they were His chosen people, and that He had made a covenant with them forever. If God were to wipe them off the face of the earth, He would be breaking covenant and denying Himself. In reality, God was just testing Moses to see if he knew God's Word or not. He wanted to know what Moses' response would be.

And to whom did he swear that they should never enter his rest, but to those who were disobedient? So we see that they were unable to enter because of unbelief (Hebrews 3:18-19 RSV).

The reason they could not enter the Promised Land was because of their murmuring, complaining, and unbelief. Their unbelief hindered the thoughts of God from coming to pass in their lives— which just so happened to be thoughts of great victory and blessing! Thankfully, unbelief has a cure. The cure is to study the Word of God and to get the thoughts of God. You have to read the Word of God out loud so that it can penetrate your mind, so that faith can come and stop unbelief. You have to deal with unbelief as early as possible and put a stop to it before it destroys what God is trying to do in your life.

Beware, brethren, lest there be in any of you an evil heart of unbelief in departing from the living God... (Hebrews 3:12).

Caleb and Joshua could see victory before them because they had not allowed discouragement, rebellion, and unbelief to silence the promise of God in their hearts. They knew that the battle was the Lord's and that He had already won it. He was basically showing them what was keeping them from experiencing both the fullness of God and the thoughts of God. With lack of vision came fear, doubt, confusion, and strife, as the children of Israel wanted to kill Joshua and Caleb for their words of belief. The Bible teaches us that God is a warrior (see Jer. 20:11) that should be dreaded by all who oppose Him. The Spirit of a warrior was not present except in Caleb and Joshua. The Israelites were not choosing to meditate on God's mighty power and acts, which they had witnessed. They had seen God's faithfulness all through the wilderness, but they did not act upon what they knew in their hearts about God. When it came time to take the land, they were unable to see God's faithfulness.

Your obedience to God's Word
determines the speed and
accuracy of your victory.

Confession will set landmarks for our life. It will set goals that lead to the right avenues. This is true, especially in the area of Kingdom finances. God wants to give us vision concerning producing finances for the Kingdom of God. Speaking prophetically, the Lord is revealing key business strategies to both men and women in the Body of Christ right now that have the potential to produce billions of dollars for the purpose of winning souls. At first these strategies are just thoughts. We have to begin to confess what God is showing us about the future in prayer. As we confess what God has revealed to us, we will begin to see God bringing His Words to pass in our lives.

MORE TO SAY ON THE CURIOUS MIND

Several times in the Bible and especially throughout the Book of Psalms people are referred to as trees. Jesus also speaks often using the analogy of a tree. Jesus told His disciples that you will know a tree by its fruit. It is not possible for a good tree to produce bad fruit; nor is it possible for a bad tree to produce good fruit. Jesus even tells a parable in Luke chapter 8 concerning what God will do with those trees that do not produce fruit:

> *He also spoke this parable: "A certain man had a fig tree planted in his vineyard, and he came seeking fruit on it and found none. Then he said to the keeper of his vineyard, 'Look, for three years I have come seeking fruit on this fig tree and find none. Cut it down; why does it use up the ground?' But he answered and said, 'Sir let it alone this year also, until I dig around it and fertilize it. And if it bears fruit, well. But if not, after that you can cut it down'"* (Luke 13:6-9).

It is obvious from these verses and others that God is expecting His children to bear good fruit. Paul tells us that we must choose whether we will be vessels of honor or vessels of dishonor (see 2 Tim. 2:20-21). We see this choice demonstrated in the Garden of Eden. The second chapter of Genesis tells us that God gave them of every good tree to eat. Verse 9 says that the tree of life was also in the Garden of Eden. This was one of the trees from which Adam and Eve could freely eat. Within the garden, God had presented His children with a choice: will you eat of the tree of the knowledge of good and evil, or will you eat of the tree of life? Christians today are also presented with this choice: will we choose to partake of satan's principles of rebellion and death, or will we choose to partake of God's Word and life? This is a decision that we make every day, continually choosing to do and become God's will on the earth. Each Christian must continue to choose to serve God—the enemy will not stop coming after you merely because you chose one day to do God's will. The decision you make will determine the product you produce. Your decision will either set a precedence for life or a precedence for death. The bottom line is, you have to feed on the tree of life. There is nothing hidden which will not be revealed. Jesus knew all things; He understood the heart of man. While you were being carefully formed in your mother's womb, God knew you. God knows what you will think before you even think it. God made you in His image and in His likeness, which included the ability to choose and proclaim life, in your thoughts, your words, and your actions. God has made it your responsibility to set your mind toward God's will.

You have the power to regulate your atmosphere.

Most scientists say that only 10 percent of the mind operates while the remaining 90 percent sits dormant. Why is that? It is because the brain is in a fallen state. Adam and Eve were just like God in all respects. They were not in a fallen state until after they sinned. Adam and Eve had the thoughts of God. They had 100 percent mind capacity. God is calling us back to the perfection He originally ordained for us. That is what the redemptive work of the Cross and resurrection of Jesus Christ is for: to bring us back to the place of oneness with God.

Adam and Eve had a God-given desire to be just like their Father God. Remember, God gave them curiosity so that they would seek for Him as for fine silver and gold. I believe, however, that when we stop satiating our desire for God with more of Him, we will begin to seek satisfaction elsewhere. Curiosity is not negative—it was created by God for God's purposes. It was meant to create a desire for exploration of God's mind and being. It is in the concept of God's mind

From Meditation to Mentality

and of God's very nature to enjoy new things. What does God want us to be curious about? God wants our curiosity focused in the direction of His plan, purpose, and vision for our lives. He wants us to be curious about knowing Him and being like Him.

Curiosity can be a powerful force for change and transformation. We do not need the curiosity of the world; this curiosity is centered on self-satisfying, self-willed desires, which lead to devising and plotting wickedness, and hurting others. As we discussed earlier, we must take those thoughts captive to the obedience of Christ. Satan will always try to throw thoughts into your head, thoughts whose purpose is to drive you out of God's arms and toward the desires of the flesh. Do not be discouraged. God has given you dominion over every enemy. You have a right and a duty to enforce God's Kingdom wherever you go. You have a privilege to control what is happening around you by speaking the Word over your world.

*God wants us focused in the right direction so that
He can bring forth creative thoughts, creative dreams,
and creative visions.*

You have a responsibility as a child of God not to allow others to dictate your atmosphere. Every day, we Christians are surrounded by ungodly influences that try to work their way into our thinking and acting. We must choose to take authority over words that are spoken to us and over us that are not from God. It is of the flesh to desire what the world offers and calls good. Selfishness continually wants more; the selfish appetite, the carnality, and evil desire of the flesh will always try to find a way to get new ideas to feed the sin. That is what the philosophers were doing when Paul came to them in the Book of Acts.

*So he argued in the synagogue with the Jews and the
devout persons, and in the market place every day with*

those who chanced to be there. Some also of the Epicurean and Stoic philosophers met him. And some said, "What would this babbler say?" Others said, "He seems to be a preacher of foreign divinities"—because he preached Jesus and the resurrection. And they took hold of him and brought him to the Areopagus, saying, "May we know what this new teaching is which you present? For you bring some strange things to our ears; we wish to know therefore what these things mean." Now all the Athenians and the foreigners who lived there spent their time in nothing except telling or hearing something new (Acts 17:17-21 RSV).

Can you see that the leaders of Greece were full of curiosity? They were just itching for something new to tickle their ears. They had developed their curiosity into an art.

If what you are meditating on is not establishing, moving, or building the creative power of God in you, you need to eliminate it. This is the standard of God's thoughts.

New ideas and concepts are not bad; in fact, God is always speaking to people and touching their lives in new and amazing ways. He did this all throughout the Bible and is still moving in people today. Yet we cannot just seek the hand of God. We must seek His face! We must love Him, not for what He can give us—He gives us all we have, without Him we would not breathe! We must love Him for who He is. Enjoy Him and seek more of Him. He wants our eyes and ears open to and focused on what He wants to bring forth in and through us.

Remember that God commanded Abraham to meditate on the stars so that he could see past death and see what belonged to him through God, to receive all that God had for him. If God's children will meditate on God's bigness, His bigness will begin to manifest in power through us.

Anything that impedes the tenderness of your conscience, obscures your sense of God, dulls your deep desire of spiritual things, or exalts the will of the flesh above the Spirit is sin. God wants to establish creative thoughts in you that will take you out of the realm of self and into the timeless eternal realms of God.

LET THE MENTALITY OF GOD RULE AND REIGN IN YOU

Thoughts establish a mindset, and mindset dictates mentality. Let your mentality be renewed through the washing of the water by the Word and let God's greatness take over in your thoughts. If you are having trouble picturing God as a healer, spend time meditating on the miracles of Jesus and Paul. If you are having trouble receiving God's love or forgiveness, meditate on Scripture verses that will reinforce what God says about you and what He sees in you. Psalm 139 is a great chapter to meditate on:

"O Lord, You have searched me and known me. You know my sitting down and my rising up; You understand my thought afar off. You comprehend my path and my lying down, and are acquainted with all my ways. For there is not a word on my tongue, but behold, O Lord, You know it altogether. You have hedged me behind and before, and laid Your hand upon me. Such knowledge is too wonderful for me; it is high, I cannot attain it. For You formed my inward parts; You covered me in my mother's womb. I will praise You, for I am fearfully and wonderfully made; marvelous are Your works, and that my soul knows very well. How precious also are Your

thoughts to me, O God! How great is the sum of them! If I should count them, they would be more in number than the sand; when I awake, I am still with You (Psalm 139:1-6,13-14,17-18).

We need to have the thoughts, the mindset, and the mentality of the supernatural. This demands that we meditate upon things above, as Colossians chapter 3 says. We must set our minds on things above and not beneath. We are no longer bound by sin, nor do we lean on the arm of the flesh. We walk in the Spirit and do not fulfill the lusts of the flesh. Do not trust in the world's solutions because God's Word is what will make lasting results of transformation and power.

We can always trust that worship and praise are going to move us nearer to God's heart. He inhabits the praises of His people. If we just come into His gates with thanksgiving and into His courts with praise, He will fill our minds with the glory of God, and we will be healed. Develop a habit of worshiping God daily, and you will find clarity in your mind. When I worship God, it causes all wrong thoughts to freeze and stop, and my mind begins to focus on loving and adoring the One who died for me and lives forever! Before you know it, the power of God will inhabit your praises, and the anointing will begin to work in your mind. This is a great tool God has given us in order to take our thoughts captive to the things of God and cast down vain imaginations and ungodly thoughts.

Consistently abiding in the presence of God and turning your mind heavenward will cause the peace of God to rule in you. Consistently think the thoughts of God by repeating the Scripture over and over in your mind. Always remember that the thoughts of the diligent tend to plenteousness. When those thoughts are further directed by the Holy Spirit, it will lead to demonstrations of greater power that will transform your life and the lives of others.

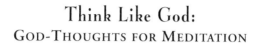

Think Like God:
GOD-THOUGHTS FOR MEDITATION

- Your meditation always becomes your mentality.
- Your meditation will affect how you view all of creation.
- Your obedience to God's Word determines the speed and accuracy of your victory.
- You have the power to regulate your atmosphere.
- God wants us focused in the right direction so that He can bring forth creative thoughts, creative dreams, and creative visions.
- If what you are meditating on is not establishing, moving, or building the creative power of God in you, you need to eliminate it. This is the standard of God's thoughts.

Chapter Eight

In Right Relationship

But when they arrest you and deliver you up, do not worry beforehand, or premeditate what you will speak. But whatever is given you in that hour, speak that; for it is not you who speak, but the Holy Spirit (Mark 13:11).

In the last seven chapters, I have been setting you up for a supernatural takeover of your consciousness by the Holy Spirit. I expect that when you are finished reading this book, your mind and your mouth will be on the road to total transformation: when you open your mouth, it will be the Word of God that comes forth; when you open your mouth, it will be the thoughts of the Most High that will be birthed! When you speak, God will administer the things that He desires to administer; it will no longer be your words. Romans chapter 8, verse 26, tells us,

> *Likewise the Spirit also helps in our weaknesses. For we do not know what we should pray for as we ought, but the Spirit Himself makes intercession for us with groanings which cannot be uttered.*

This verse is a promise from the Holy Spirit, that even while we speak, He will be speaking. When I minister in churches, I can feel the Holy Spirit within me praying in an unknown tongue, even as I preach in English. I feel as if the spirit within me goes into autopilot, and begins to declare the voice of God. Even as I speak the Word, the Holy Spirit within me is groaning, speaking those things that are not as though they were, and bringing forth the clear answer from God. You should know that while you pray in the Spirit, the Holy Spirit within you is declaring the Word of God over your circumstances. He is declaring the will of the Father over your problem. That is why many times when I am praying in the Spirit, I declare over myself:

Thank You, Father, that I receive the full manifestation of that which I am declaring in the Spirit.

You must rightfully take hold of what you speak in the Spirit, because it is the voice of God—the perfect will of the Father.

HUMILITY

I spoke briefly in an earlier chapter on the subject of humility; however, I want to take an in-depth look at what the Scripture says about God-ordained humility. Humility, according to many religious people, means to deny who God has made you to be and what God has called you to accomplish. I have even met people who say, "I want God to use me. But I'm not sure if it is God's will for me to do great things for Him or not. I do not want to go against God's will by seeking something that He does not want me to have." This is absolutely ridiculous! When I hear nonsense like this, I respond with these verses:

*If you are **willing and obedient**,*
You shall eat the good of the land; (Isaiah 1:19).

Also, I heard the voice of the Lord, saying:

"Whom shall I send,
And who will go for Us?"
*Then I said, **"Here am I! Send me"** (Isaiah 6:8-9).*

We want you to know, brethren, about the grace of God
which has been shown in the churches of Macedonia,
for in a severe test of affliction, their abundance of joy
and their extreme poverty have overflowed in a wealth
*of liberality on their part. For they gave **according to***
their means, as I can testify, and beyond their
***means, of their own free will...** (2 Corinthians*
8:1-3 RSV).

And he said to them, "Go into all the world and preach
the gospel to every creature. He who believes and is
baptized will be saved; but he who does not believe will
*be condemned. And **these signs will follow those who***
***believe:** in My name they will cast out demons; they will*
speak with new tongues; they will take up serpents, and
if they drink anything deadly, it will not hurt them; they
will lay their hands on the sick, and they will recover"
(Mark 16:15-18).

It is obvious from these verses that God is looking for a willing heart—a heart that desires to do for the Kingdom, even above and beyond its natural ability. It is not humility to deny what God has placed on the inside of you. Psalm 37:4 says, "Delight yourself in the Lord, and He will give you the desires of your heart." The desires that line up with God's Word, that are hidden in the heart, are placed there by God so that He can fulfill them. Denying a God-given desire is arrogance against God, because it is saying that you do not want what God wants. Humility is recognizing the hand of God is upon your life to bring forth His will.

Humble yourselves therefore under the mighty hand of
God, that He may exalt you in due time (1 Peter 5:6).

The Bible never instructs us to humble ourselves under a weak or wimpy hand. The Bible does not say to humble yourself under a hand that is incapable of doing anything.

Submit yourself to God's omnipotence.
This is the place of humility.

First Peter 5:6, says, "Therefore humble yourselves under the mighty hand of God, that He may exalt you in due time...." When I look at the people in the Scripture who flowed in signs and wonders, also men and women throughout history whom God has used in this way, they have all exhibited great humility and submission to the Holy Spirit. I myself, as I have grown in humility and obedience to God's Spirit, have experienced more and more signs and wonders in my own ministry. For example, a couple of years back, God instructed me to go on a trip with my spiritual father, Pastor Larry Gordon. I traveled with him to Siberia, and served him there. Because I was obedient and served my spiritual leadership, God led a mighty woman of God to prophesy over my life. She told me that when I returned home, I would experience six weeks in which everyone that I prayed for would be healed. After I got back to the United States, I experienced just what she had prophesied. Because I humbled myself and served, God blessed me, the ministry, and the hundreds of people that I prayed for.

I am the Lord: that is My name,
And My glory I will not give to another,
Nor My praise to carved images (Isaiah 42:8).

When I see God's glory truly manifesting through a human

being, I know it is because God will receive all praise, adoration, and exaltation from it. Pride wants to take credit for what God is doing. Pride wants to get the glory instead of giving it to the One who truly deserves it, the Father. I believe that God protects His glory. He does not promote people who will become puffed up with what God is doing through them. First Timothy chapter 3 tells us what God wants in church leadership. Paul specifically tells Timothy not to promote young Christians, because they may become prideful. "...Not a novice, lest being puffed up with pride he fall into the same condemnation as the devil." True humility is a place of great power. I have heard my grandfather define the word *meek* as:

Mighty, educable, emotionally stable, and kind.

To be meek is not to be in a place of great weakness, but just the opposite. When a person has moved into the realm of humility, we can expect that he or she will be able to release the love of God through finances, signs, wonders, miracles, servanthood, and in many other ways.

> *For thus says the High and Lofty One who inhabits eternity, whose name is Holy: "I dwell in the high and holy place, with him who has a contrite and humble spirit, to revive the spirit of the humble, and to revive the heart of the contrite ones"* (Isaiah 57:15).

Humble people are not stingy. Humble people are not so proud that they will not serve in simple ways. Humble people can serve tables and raise the dead. A truly humble person understands that they are submitted under El Shaddai:

> The title *Shaddai* really indicates the fullness and riches of God's grace, and would remind the Hebrew reader

that from God comes every good and perfect gift—that
He is never weary of pouring forth His mercies on His
people, and that He is more ready to give than they are
to receive. Bountiful expresses the sense most exactly. *El*
sets forth the might of God and the title *Shaddai* points
to the inexhaustible stores of His bounty.[1]

Humble people know that the Almighty resources of God's inexhaustible bounty is in them through the Holy Spirit, and that they
have the ability to release these resources into other people's lives.
Humble people have a mighty expectation as to the harvest they will
reap from sowing seeds of God's bountiful gift. They realize that God's
omnipotence has already made a way where there seemed to be no
way. They know that God's omnipotence has already provided everything that they need; therefore, they have no problem releasing what
they have.

*Humility produces a confidence in its possessors, based on
God's nature, which is immovable and steadfast.*

As I have traveled across the globe, I have seen many people
groups in poverty. I grew up in South Africa and was surrounded by
many people who were living in poverty. My grandfather, Bernard
Hunter, was a missionary and spent most of his life preaching in
poverty-stricken villages. As he preached the Gospel of Jesus Christ,
he saw whole communities changed. Because they received the Word
of God, people who were living in absolute poverty learned that it was
not God's will for them to starve or live in tin shacks. Christ did not
just change their hearts, He also changed their mindset. Poverty can
be produced by pride. When a person refuses to receive the truth of
God's Word concerning their finances, they will stay in the state they
are in. Many have received information that does not line up with the

Word of God, they exalt the ideas, philosophies, and traditions of men above the Word of God, and pride hinders them from stepping into the humility of God and the place of blessing. Many Christians need an adjustment in their thinking concerning finances. Listen, brother and sister, you are a son and daughter of God! You are seated in heavenly places. You are heirs and joint-heirs with Christ. Your thoughts will have to be altered in order to think from the realm of sonship. This is true humility.

100 PERCENT OBEDIENCE

"Now when they bring you to the synagogues and magistrates and authorities, do not worry about how or what you should answer, or what you should say. For the Holy Spirit will teach you in that very hour what you ought to say" (Luke 12:11-12).

Your job is not to tell the Holy Spirit what He wants to speak to others. Your job is not to decide what a person needs to hear. Your job is not to give what feels good to you. Your job is to obey! Your job is to open your mouth. His job is to fill it with words. Philip is a good example of this. I believe that one of the reasons that God translated him was God knew Philip's thoughts and knew that he would accomplish what God had sent him to do. Philip followed God's instructions and saw great fruit. Acts chapter 8 tells us that God sent him to a city of Samaria, and that whole city got saved, and there was great rejoicing in that city. That means that Philip knew his purpose and did his job. Next God caught him away in the Spirit to a man from Ethiopia. He preached to that man, baptized him, and left again. Whether it was a big commission or a small commission, Philip was obedient in all things. Within the commission that was given, there was 100 percent obedience. I believe this is why God had no problem translating Philip—He knew that Philip would carry out 100 percent obedience within the commission. Why would God want to take you to China if He cannot depend on you in your hometown? Can you get your neighbors saved? This is a good question to ask yourself. In order to be translated in the Spirit in the future, you must practice obedience now.

God has a plan to bless and use you now. You must focus your thought life on the task that God has set before you for this season. Allow God to speak to you in the here and now. This will make a great difference in your future. Do not rest in your own thoughts—rest on God's thoughts; He will teach you what to say to reach those closest to you. You have an unction from the Holy One who knows all things (see 1 John 2:20); this is part of your inheritance—the endless wisdom and knowledge of God. That is why Proverbs instructs us not to lean on our own understanding, but to acknowledge Him in all our ways. If we do this, He will direct our footsteps.

No matter what the situation or who the person is that God has called you to touch, the Holy Spirit knows exactly what to say in order to open their hearts to the Word of God. The Bible gives us many examples of men who calculated their words wisely in order to create a doorway of utterance into a person's heart. We see that the prophet Nathan did this with King David by telling him the parable of the poor man and his one ewe. As King David heard the parable, he became enraged at the rich man who stole the poor man's ewe, when the rich man already had so many. As the king's heart opened to hear the truth, Nathan turned to him and said, "You are the man!" (see 2 Sam. 12:7). God knew that David's heart could not stand injustice; therefore, he opened his heart by telling him a story of injustice. There are times when God will ask me to share my credentials with a person I am about to pray for. If they have cancer, I will relate to them some of the cancer miracles we have seen. For example, we were in Spartanburg, South Carolina, and there was an elderly woman whose neck was covered with cancerous tumors. I had the woman look me in they eye as I prayed for her. She was surrounded by family and friends who expected her to die. They were not exhibiting much faith; in fact by their body language and the looks on their faces, it seemed as if she had already died! I told her, "Just believe. Don't worry about what people have said to you. God is bigger." She looked into my eyes, and I rebuked the spirit of cancer. She returned to the doctor in the next few days, and she was completely free from cancer! The tumors just disappeared.

If the person is suffering from poor eyesight, I will tell them about the blind seeing. When visiting Brazil for three weeks of crusades last summer, a man born blind attended a meeting. He was in his 30s, and had never seen before. As he came up front for prayer, he was stooped over a cane, which he moved back and forth so not to bump into anything. His eyes were a white, opaque color with no irises. I prayed for the man and I felt the fire of God go through my hands into his eyes. The next night, the man returned and walked right up to the stage. I barely recognized him. He no longer had a cane, and his eyes were open with two brand-new blue irises! He testified that God had given him sight, and for the first time in his life he could see everything around him.

This is not to exalt me; we do not relate miracles to exalt the man; rather, when we retell the miracles which God has performed (through us or through others) this will grow faith in that person's heart. Then their hearts will be open to receive what God wants to impart to them through you.

> *Thus says the Lord God: "On that day it shall come to pass that thoughts will arise in your mind, and you will make an evil plan..."* (Ezekiel 38:10).

This verse demonstrates the power that God has to even see our thoughts. There are many places in the Hebrew Scriptures that show us God's ability to see and to delve into the thoughts of all men. Psalm

139 tells us that God knows our sitting down and our standing up; He knows what we think about, no matter where we are. Even when we think we are hiding from Him, he still sees us and knows us in an intimate and personal way. God says, "The thoughts I have toward you are for good, for a future, and for a hope." God knows the thoughts of all men and has given us access to His thoughts.

The root of sin is in the thoughts. This is important to know because, if we are confused about the root of sin, we will end up treating the symptoms instead of uprooting the cause. Jesus never dealt with the surface issues. When the woman caught in adultery was thrown at His feet, he did not see the outward accusation of the Pharisees. Instead He asked her plainly, "Who is left to accuse you?" (See John 8:10-11.) He instructed her not to sin anymore. When Zacchaeus met Jesus and invited the Lord to his house, he told Jesus, "Look, Lord, I give half of my goods to the poor; and if I have taken anything from anyone by false accusation, I restore fourfold." Immediately Jesus said to him, "Today salvation has come to your house!" (Luke 19:8-9). The reason that Jesus could look at the man and proclaim him saved was because the Lord recognized that the root evil in Zacchaeus's heart—namely, greed—had been dealt with and was gone. In Acts chapter 8 we see another excellent example of this:

> And when Simon saw that through the laying on of the apostles' hands the Holy Spirit was given, he offered them money, saying, "Give me this power also, that anyone on whom I lay hands may receive the Holy Spirit." But Peter said to him, "Your money perish with you, because you thought that the gift of God could be purchased with money! You have neither part nor portion in this matter, for your heart is not right in the sight of God. Repent therefore of this your wickedness, and pray God if perhaps the thought of your heart may be forgiven you" (Acts 8:18-22).

When Peter confronted the newly saved Simon, did Peter deal with the man's actions? No, Peter did not get caught up with what was manifesting on the outside. Instead he recognized the root issue of Simon's sin—his thoughts. He dealt with the man's heart. Peter said, the reason you did this is because you thought. Peter is making an interesting claim—namely, that he can see the heart, motive, and thoughts of this man. Remember that Hebrews 4:12 tells us that the Word of God is a discerner of the thoughts and intents of men's hearts. The Spirit of God within Peter was proclaiming the Word of God over his situation and Peter was merely obedient to speak what God was saying. Peter makes it clear that he is not the man's judge; rather, God is the judge, and it is to God that the man must repent. Peter basically tells the man, I am leaving the judgment of your spirit, and whether or not you have the ability to repent for these thoughts, in God's hands. The Amplified Version of the Bible quotes Peter as saying, "Pray that if possible, this contriving idea and thought and purpose of your heart may be removed and disregarded and forgiven you." We do not merely want this thought forgiven; we also want it removed and disregarded. If it is merely forgiven, there is no guarantee that the thought will not come back. This kind of thought is dangerous and leads toward the manipulation of God's power and anointing. It must be cast down and taken captive by the Word of God.

THE BONDAGE OF OFFENSE

There are times when other people's obedience to the Word of God has the opportunity to offend, because their obedience reveals and exposes our disobedience. It is time to really examine your heart. There may be people in your past or present (and I promise there will be some in your future!) whom God sends into your life for the very purpose of exposing your sin and helping you to get over it! It may be your pastor or your mentor; it may be a traveling evangelist that comes to your church. You need to make an adjustment in your thoughts if you are offended. Remember, there is no offense in Christ. The Bible teaches us that offenses will come our way (see Matt. 18:7); however, this does not give us the right to be offended. Many times in the Gospels Jesus warns against offense. When we are corrected by our leaders, we have to realize that if we are not corrected, we will not grow. If you are struggling with offense, the first thing to do is be quiet. Do not open your mouth, because offense has the ability to breed. Not only will you be listening to the lies of offense, but you will be sowing those lies into another person. This will develop a critical spirit not only in you, but in another. Before you know it, there will be judgment, anger, rottenness, gossip, and bitterness.

> *Offense grows in a critical spirit; a critical spirit breeds judgment; judgment's roots go deep and produce bitterness.*

It is very common that when we are offended, we will gather others around us who are offended in order to protect our offense. Every believer needs to realize that when you share an offense, you are opening a doorway for sickness and disease to enter another person's life. The Bible makes it very clear that offense is outside of covenant. Offense lies at the threshold of covenant. When you walk in offense, you are crossing the threshold and leaving covenant behind. When you step out of covenant, you become a target for the enemy. It is as if you are saying, "Go ahead, devil, hit me!" That is why the Bible teaches us to guard our hearts. The enemy is looking for a doorway to attack Christians. Satan is not out to steal your strength, your boldness, your positive attitude, your prayer language; satan is out to steal your joy because he know that the joy of the Lord is your strength. He knows that the Kingdom of God is righteousness, peace, and joy in the Holy Spirit. If he can get your joy, he already has destroyed your strength.

Remember, offense, bitterness, and criticism all start in the thoughts, and must be cast down and taken captive. Bitterness, anxiety, and worry all go against the knowledge of God. These thoughts go against the fruit of the Spirit—love, joy, peace, patience, etc.—that God wants to impart to you.

AGREEMENT

Society and some churches teach that a person should express how they feel, say what they think, and let it all out. That is a lie from satan. He wants to use our words to trap us in the cycle of unforgiveness and bitterness that comes from a wild and untamed tongue. The Bible teaches us to bring every thought that exalts itself in our minds into obedience to the Anointed One and His anointing. There may be thoughts coming against you right now. You need to submit every thought to Christ's authority and rule. When you cast down thoughts that do not line up with God's Word, and choose to think thoughts that do line up with God's Word, you will find the anointing being exalted in your thoughts.

Offenses, judgment, and a critical spirit come against the thoughts of love that will establish a sound mind.

The Church needs to wake up to the enemy's strategy. Principalities, powers, and demons are always working on the soulish element in carnal believers. Why does the devil have this tactic? His plan is to emphasize and exaggerate the difference in people's views of the truth instead of the points at which they are in agreement. This is the cause of denominationalism in the Body of Christ. The Bible teaches us that in the last days, the prophets will see eye to eye (see Isa. 52:8). In order for prophets to see eye to eye, they must be seeing the same thing. Many false doctrines, traditions, and philosophies of men are going to have to be uprooted from the Body of Christ before this can come to pass. God is trying to bring the Body of Christ together in unity—a unity produced from common vision and holiness, not a unity of compromise.

Satan's strategy is to keep Christians from the divine covenant relationships that will bring them into the fullness of their calling. Satan hates it when we agree—he is out to break agreement to keep Christians from fulfilling divine covenant relationship. When we are in covenant with another person, it means that everything that is ours belongs to that person, and everything that belongs to that person belongs to us. Covenant creates agreement on many levels: agreement of property, agreement of purpose, agreement of heart, and agreement of thoughts. None of them will be experienced when we are constantly biting and devouring one another with our words.

There are many ways to come to the place of agreement within the Church. One way is to fast. Isaiah 58 tells us a great deal about what God expects when we fast. Remember that God does not look at outward appearances; he looks at the heart. Anything that is not birthed out of the pure love of God will not produce any kind of good fruit. In Isaiah 58, the prophet is exposing the false motives of people who were fasting at the time when he was prophesying.

> "Cry aloud, spare not, lift up your voice like a trumpet; declare to My people their transgression, to the house of Jacob their sins. Yet they seek Me daily, and delight to know My ways, as if they were a nation that did right-eousness and did not forsake the ordinance of their God; they ask of Me righteous judgments, they delight to draw near to God. 'Why have we fasted, and Thou seest it not? Why have we humbled ourselves, and Thou takest no knowledge of it?' Behold, in the day of your fast you seek your own pleasure, and oppress all your workers. Behold, you fast only to quarrel and to fight and to hit with

*wicked fist. Fasting like yours this day will not make your voice to be heard on high. Is such the fast that I choose, a day for a man to humble himself? Is it to bow down his head like a rush, and to spread sackcloth and ashes under him? Will you call this a fast, and a day acceptable to the Lord? "Is not this the fast that I choose: to loose the bonds of wickedness, to undo the thongs of the yoke, to let the oppressed go free, and to break every yoke? Is it not to share your bread with the hungry, and bring the homeless poor into your house; when you see the naked, to cover him, and not to hide yourself from your own flesh? Then shall your light break forth like the dawn, and your healing shall spring up speedily; your righteousness shall go before you, the glory of the Lord shall be your rear guard. Then you shall call, and the Lord will answer; you shall cry, and He will say, Here I am. **"If you take away from the midst of you the yoke, the pointing of the finger, and speaking wickedness,** if you pour yourself out for the hungry and satisfy the desire of the afflicted, then shall your light rise in the darkness and your gloom be as the noonday.... "If you turn back your foot from the Sabbath, from doing your pleasure on My holy day, and call the Sabbath a delight and the holy day of the Lord honorable; if you honor it, not going your own ways, or seeking your own pleasure, or **talking idly**...* (Isaiah 58:1-10,13 ESV).

These verses show us exactly what God expects from us, not only when we fast, but all the time, making our lifestyle a fast unto God. Obedience is a type of fasting, because when a person is obedient they are fasting what they may have wanted. They are fasting the desires of the flesh. That is why God has called us to a lifestyle of fasting, where we lay down our certain desires so that we can draw near to God. For example, my wife, my children, and I do not watch secular television so we can maintain a pure mind. We fast certain types of media so we can keep our mind focused on thinking God's thoughts and not get caught up with the way the world thinks. This is what God has asked us to do, so we are being obedient. Some of us need to simply fast from speaking idle and unbelieving words. Some of us need to fast from a critical spirit, pointing the finger, and speaking wickedness over others. Remember, thoughts are where seeds are birthed, and words are where seeds are planted. Ephesians 4:29 tells us, "Let no corrupt word proceed out of your mouth, but what is good for necessary edification, that it may impart grace to the hearers." Out of the abundance of the heart the mouth speaks. I promise you that your mouth is going to speak whatever you have been thinking about.

Bad thoughts bring forth bad fruit. You must get a revelation of your authority to speak either life or death with your mouth. Your thinking would be a lot bigger if you fully comprehended where you are speaking from (the heavenly places, according to Eph. 2:6), whose you are, where you are abiding and where you are seated. God has an incredible way of taking us from one realm to another very quickly in order to make an adjustment in our thinking. In Second Samuel we read the story of how King David showed kindness to Jonathan's son, Mephibosheth. It says that he brought him in to eat at the king's table. Now that Mephibosheth is sitting at the king's table, he must adjust his thinking about himself and about the king. In Second Samuel 9:6, Mephibosheth called himself David's servant. Yet just a few verses later David told him that he would sit at his table as one of his sons. To go from bring a servant to being a son, a person must change the way he or she thinks. They are no longer in bondage. They are heirs and part of the family.

Many times God brings us into a covenant relationship in order to take us to a place we have never been before. When you were in the world, you had one pattern of thinking. However, once you come into covenant with God, He says that you are seated in heavenly places. Once you are brought into covenant relationship with God, you are brought into the presence of God. Your thinking can no longer remain in the natural realm when your spirit has been lifted into the supernatural realm.. Now you are speaking as an ambassador of Christ—your words have to be calculated, precise, and accurate. Now your words carry authority. Even though a person may have a thought pass through his or her mind at times that they recognize is not of God, it does not change the fact that he or she is a child of God. When a thought that is not of God goes through our minds, it is our choice to do either what is right or what is wrong with that thought. We have been empowered by the Holy Spirit to choose God's way, instead of our own.

Jesus constantly gives us an example to follow concerning authoritative words. Many people who saw Jesus minister marked that when He spoke, Jesus did not speak like the Pharisees; for He spoke with authority. That meant His words produced results. Matthew chapter 8 tells us of the centurion whose servant was sick. He asked Jesus to merely say the word and his servant would be healed. The centurion understood that Jesus' words had authority to drastically alter his present circumstances. Jesus did not agree or disagree with the man's words. He merely said, "Go." Jesus had no pride. He did not need the accolades of men; He knew He was anointed and that the anointing had the power to remove every burden and destroy every yoke. He had nothing to prove, because the anointing proved itself.

TIME FOR ACTION

I beseech you therefore, brethren, by the mercies of God, that you present your bodies a living sacrifice, holy, acceptable to God, which is your reasonable service. And do not be conformed to this world, but be transformed by the renewing of your mind, that you may prove what is that good and acceptable and perfect will of God (Romans 12:1-2).

When we are transformed by the renewing of our minds we will be able to prove what is the good, acceptable, and perfect will of God. To have a renewed and transformed mind that can be a conduit for God's Word is God's good, acceptable, and perfect will! In order to take action in altering our thoughts, we must allow our mind to be washed with the water of the Word.

Here are some actions you can take to annihilate the strongholds of the enemy in your mind:

1. Take responsibility for your own thoughts.
2. Rethink thoughts before you speak them.
3. Line your thoughts up with the unction of the Holy Spirit.
4. Reject old thoughts. You are not living in the past. The decisions of tomorrow need tomorrow's wisdom not yesterday's or today's. Every day is new. Every day you need fresh manna, fresh thoughts from God. Many times we try to apply our experiences with past wisdom in current situations. The wisdom that is needed to operate in the supernatural comes from God alone—not from time or experience. Wisdom from lifetime experiences can shut down the supernatural.
5. Remember, tomorrow will be a new day of thought. This will maintain our desire to receive fresh input from God each day. Fresh manna is what gives us strength for the new day. That is why it is important to establish a habitual intimacy with God's Word. Memorizing Scriptures helps to create great inner fortitude that will carry you through tough times. One Scripture can keep you healed for the rest of your life. If you allow the Word of God to take on flesh in your heart, it

will open the door for God's life to spring forth speedily.

Remember that God's promises are covenant principles. Outside of covenant, these promises will have no effect in your life. God said, if you obey My covenant, you will be blessed; if you disobey My covenant, you will be cursed. Remember that envy and self-seeking are outside of covenant. This kind of thinking is outside of God's pattern. When our thinking gets outside of the covenant thoughts of God, confusion will come in. James teaches us that if we want to see our prayers answered and much power available to us, then we have to deal with envy, strife, self-seeking, and rebellion, the wisdom that is demonic.

In Luke chapter 4, Jesus is tempted in the spirit, the soul, and the body. Before He could enter into ministry in the power of the Holy Spirit, He went through a massive attack from the enemy that tested the Word of God in Jesus. You see, before we can truly enter into the power available to us through the Holy Spirit, we must deal with the trash that stands between us and covenant. Jesus never cast out any devils, healed any sick person, nor raised anyone from the dead until He was tempted. Once He passed the three temptations, He came out of the wilderness in the power of the Holy Spirit.

The sooner you deal with the flesh, the appetites and the lusts of it, the quicker the thoughts of God, the mind of Christ, and the power of the Spirit will rule and reign in your life.

We see this principle even operated in Jesus' life. Now go back with me to James chapter 4. What does the apostle expose about the desires of our hearts? "You lust and do not have [you want it your way]. You murder and covet [I, me, my] and cannot obtain. You fight and war. Yet you do not have because you do not ask [His way]." It is either going to be your way or His way! "You ask and do not receive because you ask amiss [false motives], that you may spend it on your pleasures. Adulterers and adulteresses! Do you not know that friendship with the world is enmity with God? Whoever therefore wants to be a friend of the world makes himself an enemy of God. Or do you think that the Scripture says in vain, 'The Spirit who dwells in us yearns jealously'?" (James 4:2-5). The enemy comes to talk to the flesh, when all along it is supposed to be dead! Satan is trying to bring thoughts to the flesh when we know that it is already dead.

A church without humility, obedience, and agreement is a church without power.

A church like this has no ability to reach its community because it is outside of covenant. A church must exhibit the same nature and character that Jesus did in order to reach people. Remember that when you receive the Word of God, you must speak forth the Word and thoughts of love. Speak encouragement.

1. Pursue God's thoughts.
2. Gain the knowledge of the Anointed One's anointing—the mind of Christ.
3. Meditate on Christ's thoughts daily.
4. Resist the temptation of old, traditional, limited ways of thinking.
5. Do not lean on your own understanding and thoughts, but lean on God's thoughts. Remember that as your thoughts are, so shall your life be. Your life is a direct consequence of your thinking.
6. Renew your mind on the Word of God.

7. Maintain a continual atmosphere of praise and worship.

Right now I speak a blessing over everyone that is reading this book. I thank You, Father, that You teach Your children how to line up every wrong thought that attacks their minds with God's desires for their lives through Your Word. I thank You, Father, that before our thoughts escape our mouths, God will show every person in their minds how to attain God's thoughts. I thank You, Father, that they think and speak in alignment with the unction of the Holy Spirit. Father, I thank You for the blood of Christ that purges their consciences from every dead, wrong, and negative thought, every thought that goes against the Word of God, every thought that is contrary to the supernatural working of the Holy Spirit. I thank You, Father, in the name of Jesus, that the blood of Jesus purges their consciences from all dead works, any idea that does not bring life, any thought that does not bring strength and health to their bodies. Purge it out, Lord, right now, in Jesus' name!

I thank You, Father, that they have an unction from the Holy One who knows all things, that they have an anointing that abides in them and teaches them all things. I thank You, God, that they will think Your thoughts, that they will speak Your thoughts. I thank You, Father, that they do not speak their own words, but they will only speak the Words of their Father in Heaven. I thank You, Father, that they are absolutely dependent on You. I thank You, Father, that they have the mind of Christ, that they have an anointed mind, that they think anointed thoughts and they speak anointed words, and everything they do produces anointed results. I thank You, Father, that the anointing is manifest in every circumstance of their lives; because anointed thoughts are going to crystallize and solidify into anointed habits that are going to produce anointed circumstances. Creative thoughts are going to solidify into habitual creative thinking; I thank You, Father, that these thoughts are going to manifest in the creative power of God ruling and reigning in their lives.

I thank You, Father, that they are ambassadors of Christ, that they are seated in heavenly places. I thank You that their thoughts line up with their position. I thank You that they think like a son and daughter of God. They talk like a son and daughter of God. They walk like a son and daughter of God. I thank You, Father, that they cast out devils like a son and daughter of God; they heal the sick and raise the dead like a son and daughter of God, because they are sons and daughters of God! I thank You that the revelation of God's thoughts manifests in every action that they do, in the name of Jesus.

I ask You, Father, to have your rule and reign in them! Manifest Your fullness through them. Let the anointing that You have given them, that You have placed inside this earthen vessel, the treasure of the Holy Spirit, let it rule and reign. Let Christ in them be the hope of glory. Let the anointing in them be responsible to produce the glory. Let the anointing within them be responsible to remove burdens and destroy yokes. Let the anointing in them be responsible to administer the healing anointing, right now in the name of Jesus! They are anointed! They are full of the power of

God! They are the head and not the tail! They are the King's children.

Thank You, Lord, that they have been clothed with the power of God; thank You that they have been clothed with divine capabilities. Thank You, Lord, that they have on the robes of righteousness. Their feet are shod with the gospel of peace. They have the helmet of salvation. Their minds are girded with strength. They have absolute security, soundness, wholeness, and peace in their minds. Their minds are filled with the consciousness of God, the peace of God rules and reigns in their minds, and they speak from the realm of peace. Thank You, Lord, that when they speak to the river, peace will be the result. Thank You, Father, that they administer the peace of God where they walk, in their talk, and in their actions.

Thank You that they think like You, Heavenly Father! I thank You that they think like the omnipotent, omniscient, omnipresent One. Thank You, Father, that as they think, supernatural things begin to happen; Thank You, Father, that the mind of God rules and reigns in everything they do. Thank You, Father, for the Kingdom of God that has come and lives within them: righteousness, peace, and joy in the Holy Spirit. Thank You, Father, that they meditate on things that are pure, wholesome, healthy, righteous, encouraging, uplifting, in Jesus' name! I thank You that they Think Like God!

Think Like God:
GOD-THOUGHTS FOR MEDITATION

- Thank You, Father, that I receive the full manifestation of that which I am declaring in the Spirit.
- Submit yourself to God's omnipotence. This is the place of humility.
- Meek: mighty, educable, emotionally stable, and kind.
- Humility produces a confidence in its possessors, based on God's nature, which is immovable and steadfast.
- Offense grows in a critical spirit; a critical spirit breeds judgment; judgment's roots go deep and produce bitterness.
- The sooner you deal with the flesh, the appetites and the lusts of it, the quicker the thoughts of God, the mind of Christ, and the power of the Spirit will rule and reign in your life.
- A church without humility, obedience, and agreement is a church without power.

ENDNOTE

1. James Strong, *The New Strong's Expanded Exhaustive Concordance of the Bible: Strong's Expanded Hebrew and Aramaic Dictionary* (Nashville, TN: Thomas Nelson Publishers, 2001), 272.

Author and Ministry Information

Sword Ministries

PO Box 7360

Branson, MO 65615

WWW.SWORDMINISTRIES.ORG

Become a carrier of REVIVAL!

God wants you to preach His Gospel with the **power** and **demonstration of the Holy Spirit**. Join Apostolic Revivalist Warren Hunter in "Supernatural Leadership Training Institute: School of the Revivalist!"

Apostolic Revivalist Warren Hunter will train you, through **21 DVD training sessions**, to minister in the power of the Holy Spirit with signs and wonders following. Included with the 21 DVD set is the **School of the Revivalist Training Manual**.

Within the training manual are **outlines for each DVD as well as 21 outworking assignments**. This school is not designed for the Sunday pew sitter. After you complete the 21 DVDs and the assignments, you will be ministering in the power of God to your friends, family, and community!

License and ordination are available upon meeting predetermined requirements.

Order now for $495.00 by calling 417-335-7650 or visiting www.swordministries.org.

SUPERNATURAL
LEADERSHIP
TRAINING
INSTITUTE

Prophetically designed with YOU in mind,
this school will empower YOU
to do the impossible for God.
With over 20 specialized DVD teachings
and corresponding manual,
YOU have the tools
to readily learn how to
effectively minister
the Word of God with
Signs and Wonders
following
to the
Nations
of the world!

For more information visit